Managing Middle School Madness

Helping Parents and Teachers Understand the "Wonder Years"

Glen Gilderman

D1714141

Rowman & Littlefield Education
Lanham • New York • Toronto • Plymouth, UK

Published in the United States of America
by Rowman & Littlefield Education
A Division of Rowman & Littlefield Publishers, Inc.
A wholly owned subsidiary of The Rowman & Littlefield Publishing
Group, Inc.
4501 Forbes Boulevard, Suite 200, Lanham, Maryland 20706
www.rowmaneducation.com

Estover Road
Plymouth PL6 7PY
United Kingdom

British Library Cataloguing in Publication Information Available

Library of Congress Cataloging-in-Publication Data

Gilderman, Glen, 1965–
  Managing middle school madness : helping parents and teachers
understand the "wonder years" / Glen Gilderman.
      p. cm.
  Includes bibliographical references and index.
  ISBN-13: 978-1-57886-515-4 (cloth : alk. paper)
  ISBN-10: 1-57886-515-8 (cloth : alk. paper)
  ISBN-13: 978-1-57886-516-1 (pbk. : alk. paper)
  ISBN-10: 1-57886-516-6 (pbk. : alk. paper)
  1. Middle school education—Parent participation. 2. Middle school
teaching. I. Title.
  LB1623.G5 2007
  373.236—dc22   2006016505

♾™ The paper used in this publication meets the minimum requirements
of American National Standard for Information Sciences—Permanence of
Paper for Printed Library Materials, ANSI/NISO Z39.48-1992.
Manufactured in the United States of America.

Contents

Preface

This is coming from a teacher, but . . .

It might be interesting for you to know that I have been a parent of a middle school / junior high student, and I do teach or come into contact with about four hundred 7th- and 8th-graders per year. I am utterly amazed at how unprepared parents seem to be for this very tumultuous time.

The problem I hear from parents is that their children metamorphosed over the summer, and they don't know them any more! This is not the parents' or child's fault. It is part of a move toward independence and autonomy that every normal child must pass through in order to become a healthy adult. The problem is that this child moving toward independence makes the parent(s) feel like an unhealthy adult!

The following chapters are an attempt to make these times easier. My experience comes from sitting with perplexed parents at parent/teacher conferences, talking about and witnessing successful techniques used by effective parents and foster parents, and working with a broad range of children.

I spent the first part of my teaching career working with emotionally or behaviorally disordered children in a Junior High Alternative Center, Residential Treatment Centers, and an Adolescent Chemical Dependency Center. For the past thirteen years I have continued to see many of these same frustrations in the parents of the middle school social studies students I now work with. Suffice it to say, I have come in contact with many parents who were at their wits' ends. Sadly enough, some of these parents had already given up. In some cases, unconditional love had turned into unconditional rights to treat parents any way the child wanted to.

This book is about being proactive with your child. It is about trying to head the problems off at the pass. It is like reading about riding that bucking bronco before you actually try to ride it. I hope it helps!

Although this book is addressed to parents, I believe that it could also be a great help to teachers of middle school students. Teachers could use the contracts and worksheets when meeting with perplexed parents.

For teachers new to the middle school level, this book will give a helpful window to the inside of that world. It offers great ideas about how to work with middle school students and their parents. The statistics plug in to the trends of middle school–aged students. For teachers, too, I hope that this book makes a difference!

Acknowledgments

Thanks to my wife, Terrie, for putting up with all the late nights and being a supportive partner. Thanks also to my kids, Katie and Boston, for answering all the questions about middle school and about being a student. Professionally, thanks to Sherm Carlson, Diane Rauschenfels, Patty Muckala, Gloria McDonald, Lowell and Jen Harnell, Jim and Jamie Savre, and Shelley Maas for helping to support my efforts and for proofreading my early work.

Letter to the Parents of a Middle-schooler

Dear Mom and Dad,

Today was my first day at my new job. I have new teachers, new rooms, a new system to adjust to, new subjects, and many new friends.

With all these new beginnings, I am making many big adjustments. I have many things to remember. When I get tired, irritable, or easily upset, remember all the adjustments you had to make when you started a new job and all the fears you had—it will help you to understand how I feel.

You can help me a lot by listening sympathetically, being understanding, giving me your support, helping me to get more rest, and giving me lots of love and attention.

Thank you very much!

Love,

Your middle school son/daughter

As this writing illustrates, many changes are going to be occurring—accept that fact and cut your child a little slack!

Chapter One

Dealing with the School

A school is a building with four walls and tomorrow inside.

Barbara Knight

Being an educator, I always try to assume that you are going to be dealing with professional people at the school in which your child is enrolled. Some of the suggestions in this chapter require you to be a very involved parent. Most teachers, guidance counselors, and administrators will welcome your support and enthusiasm. For the few who will not, it's their job, so just expect it of them, and they will probably come through.

TIP #1:
Above All, See Yourself in a Partnership with the School

The following poem by an unknown author does a great job demonstrating the importance of unity in the parent/school relationship:

Unity

I dreamed I stood in a studio
And watched two sculptors there.
The clay they used was a young child's mind
And they fashioned it with care.

One was a teacher—the tools he used
Were books, music, and art.
The other, a parent, worked with a guiding hand,
And a gentle, loving heart.
Day after day, the teacher toiled with touch
That was careful, deft, and sure.
While the parent labored by his side
And polished and smoothed it o'er.

And when, at last, their task was done,
They were proud of what they had wrought.
For the things they had molded into the child
Could neither be sold or bought.

And each agreed they would have failed
If each had worked alone.
For behind the parent stood the school
And behind the teacher, the home.

TIP #2:
Orientation/Open House

Make a real effort to attend the orientation/open house with your child. The school will probably go over lots of things that may not seem like a big deal to you but are very scary to a child entering a new school.

I can't tell you how many times I have had to console a young student because he or she couldn't get his or her locker open and was going to be late for class. These students were not usually afraid of the teacher because most will cut students a lot of slack the first couple of weeks. They were afraid of entering a class late and having all the other students looking at them. Make sure your child knows:

His hourly schedule
Where his teachers' rooms are located

The number of his bus and its location at the end of the day
Where her lockers (regular and gym) are and how to work the combination locks
Where the bathrooms are
Where the office is
A teacher she can go to for questions (in a middle school, usually her advisor).

TIP #3:
Help Your Son/Daughter Set Up His/Her Schedule

During the middle school years, children are not known for using great judgment. They will probably choose a class based on which friends are in that class before they think about their educational future. Most schools send enrollment information home in the spring of the year. Letting your child fill in the classes would probably be a mistake. Sit down with the child and discuss each class.

Make a list of positives and negatives for each elective class. Even though students may have limited elective classes at this level of their education, choosing not to take band in 7th grade could limit the choices they have in the future. Let the child feel some ownership by being a partner in the decision making.

Encourage, maybe even demand, that your child take challenging classes that fit with his maturity and intelligence level. If your child is a very good reader and highly motivated, encourage him to take honors English if it is offered. One note of caution: If your child is an average or below-average reader, don't push him up a notch so he can become better. This can lead to discouragement, and the child could start to dislike reading altogether.

Try to be realistic as a parent. If your child is an underachiever, challenge her to take a tough class, but draw up a contract with rewards and consequences for success or failure.

See the appendix for a sample contract that you can use with your daughter or son. Some examples of rewards and consequences are listed below.

Possible Examples for Rewards

One Saturday off (no chores)
Parent will do one of child's chores for a week
New computer software
Movie pass
Dinner out
One ride to mall with no complaining
Parent pays child's cell phone bill for one month
Parent pays for text messaging on child's cell phone for one month
Parent purchases one ring tone for child's cell phone
Any activity of child's choice
Be creative (nonmaterial things provide longer lasting memories)

Possible Examples for Consequences

Added chores
No video games
Added structured study time
No rides to mall
Limited TV
Child is grounded from using phone
Child's cell phone is taken away
Text-messaging capability is removed from child's cell phone
Early Saturday wake-up
Earlier bedtime

Again, be creative. Try to focus on negative reinforcement (taking good things away) rather than punishment (giving bad things). The former is less likely to create a barrier. Make sure the consequences have defined, realistic time lines. Do not threaten what you will not be able to follow through with, and *by all means, follow through!*

TIP #4:
Find Out about Extra Help before the School Year Begins

Many schools have tutoring programs where students help other students. Get more information from the school. Don't assume that because your child received average and above-average grades in elementary school that junior high will be the same. Many children struggle with the huge changes in specialization and times. They may need some help to get accustomed to the new routine and the challenges that go along with the many changes they will face.

Be sure to monitor your child's progress carefully so if he is struggling, you can get him help right away. Finding out about your school's programs can open a door for volunteering if the adjustment is easy. If your school doesn't have a tutoring program, ask administrators to refer you to a reputable business in your community. If no tutoring program is available, start one!

TIP #5:
If Your Child Is Struggling: When to Look at Special Education or a 504 Plan

In my years of teaching, I have witnessed quite a few parents who resisted getting their child help through special education services. Special education today is not the same special education that you grew up with. Students are not separated from the rest of the class. They are in regular mainstream classes and are generally not singled out.

Most special education teachers have one time during the day when they meet with their students in a classroom, where they function as a resource to help students organize their work and increase study skills. For most of the day, students may see the special education teacher as a second teacher in their mainstream classes. The special education teacher will probably help any student who requires it, while spending more time helping students on their caseload. Most special education teachers will try to be seen as another adult in the room, not as one kid's special teacher.

Because of the complicated federal laws on special education, I will attempt here to give a simple description of some of the various programs designed to help children cope. As a former special education teacher who is still licensed to teach students with emotional difficulties, it strikes me as funny that I feel like I should talk to a colleague to find out how all of the acronyms have changed for this year. Instead, I will use the terms I know here to help parents decide whether they need to seek some help for their son or daughter.

All students who qualify for special education will be put on something called an Individual Educational Plan (IEP). This is a legal document that has many rules attached. If your child is put on an IEP, you will have meetings to determine progress and to plan for your child's educational future. This is an area where you can exert a lot of control over your child's education. You will be on a team with your child's regular education teachers, the special education teacher, an administrator, and any other people who are part of your child's educational life.

Learning Disabilities (LD)

What Is It?

Contrary to popular belief, a student must score as average in intelligence to qualify as learning-disabled. They must score between 90 and 110 on an IQ test to be able to receive services. There must be a significant gap between intelligence and achievement in the areas of mathematics, reading, or written expression.

I lead an activity in my classroom to demonstrate how being learning-disabled might feel. Students must hold a mirror on their desk and trace a star while only looking in the mirror. They are graded on speed and accuracy. Many students who have found school a breeze struggle mightily with this task. After the activity, I ask them how it felt to try really hard to be good at this task but still have a very difficult time. They always answer, "Frustrating."

I then ask them to consider what life might be like if the skill of tracing the star was a part of every class and it was how you were graded. That may be what is felt by someone who finds it very difficult to read, write, or do math. I hope that this activity gives my students some empathy.

What Help Is Available?

Most LD teachers work on study skills, organization, and the student-specific area of concern. They advocate for the child, suggest modifications of lessons to mainstream teachers, and assist the student with tests. Their job is to follow the IEP.

Emotional/Behavioral Disorders (EBD)

What Is It?

EBD is for students who are experiencing behavior issues in school. The behavioral issues are interfering with their education and with the other students in the school. The purpose of the program is to help the student learn to behave and to get along with their peers and teachers. For the first four years of my career I taught EBD students in many settings. I taught in residential treatment centers, alternative schools, and regular schools.

I observed that students who were EBD were angry, scared, or bored. Some of these students had very tough home lives. Some had been abused. Some were mentally ill. Some were spoiled brats.

Some were so smart that not being challenged was causing them to act out. Some struggled with learning disabilities, dyslexia, or Attention Deficit Disorder. And some were kids who came from normal families who could not figure out what was wrong.

What Help Is Available?

Your child basically will be given the services he or she needs to function in a regular classroom. Your child will also receive an IEP, which can focus on behavior and academic areas. Your child's case manager will advocate for him or her and will work with coping techniques so the child can find success. The case manager will help the mainstream teacher with adaptations, interventions, and accommodations.

Mild/Moderate Mental Impairment (MMMI)

What Is It?

This is an acronym that seems to constantly change depending on political correctness. This special education area is for children who have lower than average IQs. For some reason, they have a low IQ and need some extra help in school. These students will usually have some core classes in the mainstream. One of the greatest things that MMMI students give to their classmates is an understanding that we are all human. Since I started teaching, I have been blessed to have taught some of the most unique people in the world.

As part of my class, I do a psychology project where students have to do a report on something to do with the brain. One of my students, Jenny, had Down syndrome. After turning in their written projects, students can do an oral presentation for extra credit.

Jenny did her project on Down syndrome and was very excited to present her project. It was one of the most amazing moments I have ever experienced. She took the opportunity to explain to her class-mates her struggles and the great things about being who she was. She explained that the reason she had a tough time talking was be-cause her tongue was a little too big. She explained her heart sur-geries. She explained that it was harder for her to learn, but she tried really hard and she was making great progress. The presentation was a great eye-opener for my class.

What Help Is Available?

MMMI teachers help their students to function in school and life. They teach them the needed skills to thrive. They often set up jobs outside of school to teach occupational and social skills.

Other Health Impaired (OHI)

What Is It?

OHI is kind of a catchall for other health impaired. It could include ADD or ADHD, asthma, diabetes, and other conditions that adversely affect the child's education.

What Help Is Available?

It depends on the problem, but school districts are responsible for educating all children, regardless of disability. They are also respon-sible for educational accommodations.

Other Categories of Special Education

Visual Impairment
Speech or Language Impairment
Traumatic Brain Injury
Orthopedic Impairment

Hearing Impairment
Autism

504 Plans

If your child does not fit into a special education category, but is still struggling in school, you may want to look at something called a 504 plan.

A 504 plan is a legal document included in the Rehabilitation Act of 1973. It is for planning a program for students who may have some sort of disability, but do not fall into special education guidelines. A 504 plan is not an Individualized Education Program (IEP) that I mention above for special education students.

If your child has a physical or emotional disability or has an impairment (Attention Deficit Disorder, diabetes) that restricts learning, he or she will probably qualify for a 504 plan. In order to be placed on a 504 plan, the student must be referred by a teacher, support staff, parent/guardian, or someone from the medical community. After referral, a committee meeting of people involved in the child's learning (student, teachers, principal, nurse, counselor, and anyone else you want to invite) must be held and a plan developed.

During this meeting, the committee should discuss any accommodations that would aid the student in their learning process. The accommodations should be tied to the disability. Some examples could be the location of their seats in their classrooms, or being able to leave the classroom with a partner to check blood and to eat in class for a diabetic. As in an IEP, teachers could be told to modify tests by giving more time.

As a parent, you may be asked to assist at home in some way to help with the 504 plan. Setting a specific bedtime or setting aside a certain amount of study time could be a part of the plan.

The plan can be changed at the request of anyone on the team. To change the plan, another meeting must be called. A yearly review should be done to assess the effectiveness of all accommodations.

TIP #6:
Encourage Your Child to Ask the Teacher about Extra Credit, Enrichments, or Anything Else He or She Can Do to Help a Grade

As a teacher, I am always impressed when a student asks me if there is anything he or she can do to improve his or her grade. Knowing students really care about the grade they get makes me feel like they are willing to go the extra mile, and I will reward them for this. There is, however, a difference between asking for extra work and asking if I know what their grade is.

With about 150 students during a typical year, I do not have time to subtotal grades to find out if a student *needs* to do extra work. Knowing that a student will only do extra work if he or she has to gives me the impression that the student will just do enough to get by. Asking for work without asking for a grade means a student doesn't care if he or she already has an "A." Such students are still willing to do work to make sure they can improve their grade. I have grade sheets posted all through the year (anonymously) so students can note their progress. Students who are constantly checking them impress me because they are showing that they are conscientious.

TIP #7:
Is Your Child Gifted?

According to my research, there is not a great answer to that question. Most experts in this area use the 5 percent rule as a benchmark. If your child scores in the top 5 percent on a standardized IQ test, they *could* be considered gifted. I have taught quite a few students that I would consider gifted but have never been told to do anything different with them.

Most teachers will find extra activities to challenge a gifted student. This should not be busywork, but work that stretches the bounds of the student's intelligence. Frankly, I have learned a lot from my gifted students by assigning them to look into an area of interest and thereby expanding my own knowledge!

At the end of this book, I list a few websites that may help you to determine if your child is gifted and what to do about it.

TIP #8:
Highly Encourage Your Child to Get Involved in Some Sort of Extracurricular Activity

Extracurricular activities add a different perspective to any student's educational experience. They teach students the value of self-discipline, perseverance, hard work, and in many cases, teamwork. These activities give them a chance to meet new friends (generally the kinds of kids that are in extracurriculars are the type of children you want your child to befriend) and help them learn to work with people they don't really like. This could be coaches, advisors, or other participants.

Statistics That Back Up the Value of Participation

Of the sixty students listed in the May 14, 1998, *USA Today*'s All-USA High School Academic First, Second, and Third Teams and the fifty-one who earned honorable mention, 75 percent were involved in sports, speech, music, or debate.

In a survey of 4,800 high school students in March 1995, the Minnesota State High School League found that 91 percent of them said students who participate in school activities tend to be school leaders and role models; 92 percent said that participation in school activities provides an opportunity not found in a regular classroom setting to develop self-discipline.

"Adolescent Time Use, Risky Behavior, and Outcomes: An Analysis of National Data," issued in September 1995 by the Department of Health and Human Services, found that students who spend no time in extracurricular activities are 57 percent more likely to have dropped out of school by the time they would have been seniors; 49 percent more likely to have used drugs; 37 percent more likely to have become teen parents; 35 percent more likely to have smoked cigarettes; and 27 percent more likely to have been arrested than those who spend one to four hours per week in extracurricular activities.

Research conducted in 1991 by Skip Dane of Hardiness Research, Casper, Wyoming, revealed the following about participation in high school sports:

1) By a two-to-one ratio, boys who participate in sports do better in school, do not drop out, and have a better chance to get through college.
2) The ratio for girls who participate in sports and do well in school is three to one.
3) About 92 percent of sports participants do not use drugs.
4) Student athletes are more self-assured.
5) Sports participants take average and above-average classes.
6) Sports participants receive above-average grades and do above average on skills tests.
7) Those involved in sports have knowledge of and use financial aid and have a chance to finish college.
8) Student athletes appear to have more parental involvement than other students.
9) Students involved in athletics appear to change focus from cars and money to life accomplishments during the process.

A study of nearly 22,000 students conducted by a University of Colorado professor for the Colorado High School Activities Association released in fall 1999 indicates students who participate in some form of interscholastic activities have "significantly higher" grade-point averages than students who do not.

Data obtained from the spring 1997 study by Dr. Kevin J. Mc-
Carthy revealed student participants in Jefferson County high
schools had an overall grade-point average of 3.093 on a 4.0 scale,
while the GPA for nonparticipants was 2.444. Jefferson County
School District, Colorado's largest school district, has matched the
academic success of its students with success on the playing field.
The sixteen district schools won a combined thirty-nine state cham-
pionships in the 1990s in sports, while its music programs consistently bring home "superior" ratings.

In a comprehensive, statewide study of the academic performance
of high school student athletes in North Carolina over a three-year
period, the North Carolina High School Athletic Association found
significant differences between athletes and nonathletes. Five crite-
ria were used, including grade-point average, attendance rate, discipline referrals, dropout rate, and graduation rate, for the 1994–1995
academic year.

According to the Minnesota State High School League:

Decades of research prove that students who participate in high
school activities tend to have higher grade-point averages, better attendance records, lower dropout rates, and fewer discipline problems than nonparticipating students.

National studies repeatedly report that high school activities build
character, increase self-confidence, relieve tension, and support
classroom learning by generating school pride and a sense of com-

Table 1.1.   Comparing the Performance of Student Athletes and Nonathletes

	Athletes	Nonathletes
Grade-point average	2.86	1.96
Average number of absences per 180-day school year	6.52 days	12.57 days
Discipline referrals	30.51%	40.29%
Dropout rate	0.7%	8.98%
Graduation rate	99.56%	94.66%

Source: Reprinted with permission of the National Federation of State High School Associations, Jan-
uary 2006.

munity, and by nurturing a feeling of belonging that makes students want to achieve.

These studies also show that students who participate in athletic and fine arts programs are more likely to graduate from high school, stay off drugs, attend college, and avoid unwanted pregnancies. Still more statistics reveal that participation in activities encourages the aspirations of youth and provides young people with countless opportunities to develop leadership skills.

A Minnesota study of more than three hundred schools showed:

- The average student had a grade-point average of 2.68 (on a 4.0 scale), but the grade-point average of student athletes was 2.84 and 2.98 for students involved in the fine arts—speech, drama, music, and debate.
- The average student was absent 8.76 days a year. Athletes were absent 7.44 days. Fine arts participants were absent only 6.94 days a year.

As a coach, I like to think I teach kids how to have a positive attitude, how to win and lose gracefully, and the value of working together, goal setting, and working hard, along with many other life lessons. If your child is not an athlete or is not interested in sports, encourage involvement in speech, drama, debate, yearbook, school newspaper, DECA, or any of the many other nonathletic options. Most of my fondest memories of junior high and high school are not from the classroom, but from school experiences outside the classroom.

TIP #9:
Go Through the School Handbook
Item by Item with Your Child

This is one of the best ways for your child to feel confident on the first day of school. Teachers and administrators generally spend a great deal of time working on handbooks for their students. Present this to your child as the chance to have an advantage over other students by knowing all of the rules, policies, schedules, and other very important miscellaneous information contained in school handbooks. This will also give you, as a parent, some leverage if your child breaks the rules during the year. It can put you in the position of being a well-informed parent, which teachers will appreciate. There will be no surprises if you read the handbook together from cover to cover.

Chapter Two

Dealing with the Teacher

The teacher's job is to . . .

Teach! My job as the teacher of your child is to pass on some objectives that have been predetermined by the school district. This job, however, is the tip of the iceberg. Teachers also fill the role of counselors, police officers, nurses, guards, disciplinarians, and many other jobs. I, like most other teachers, take this job very seriously. I enjoy it, and I can't see myself doing anything else.

CLASSROOM BEHAVIOR

The bottom line in my classroom and in most teachers' classrooms is that everyone has an equal opportunity to learn, and no one person has the right to interfere with any other person's opportunity. My classroom discipline is simple—interfere with another student's learning and get a consequence.

Most of the time, the consequence is a call home. Kids hate calls home . . . so do many teachers. Teachers dislike calling home because every once in a while they will run into a parent who goes on the defensive. Every parent has an idealistic perception of their child, and some parents refuse to believe that their child would ever do anything wrong. Please don't be one of those parents!

A positive relationship with your child's teacher is extremely important.

The following are some tips for great parent/teacher relationships.

TIP #1:
Handling Conflicts between a Teacher and Your Child

If your child comes home to report a situation with a teacher, outwardly back the teacher right away. Does this sound like I'm telling you not to trust your child? Well, I am, at least right away. There are very few teachers who go around looking for trouble with students. Most will not lie about a situation to get your child into trouble. When the teacher calls (if they don't call, wait a few days and call them), listen and assume they are telling the truth. If it helps, try to pretend that the teacher is talking about someone else's child. This may make the story easier to believe.

The bottom line here is that your child may lie to stay out of trouble with you. If you can think back to these years in your own life, you probably lied to your parents about something along the way. Your child is capable of the same!

I do have to acknowledge that, as in any other field, there are some bad teachers out there. I encourage you to believe the teacher unless you truly believe your child has been wronged. If you feel they have, do some more investigating. After talking to the teacher personally, call the principal to discuss the situation.

Have a heart-to-heart talk with your child, letting them know that you are going to pursue this matter. If they are lying, this will probably force them to tell the truth. Let them know about consequences, like tarnishing one's good name. Let them know that if you advocate for them and they are lying, the consequences will be strong.

If they are not lying, it might be one of the greatest things you could do for your child and any other child who will have contact with this teacher in the years to come.

TIP #2:
How to Treat a Teacher in a Conflict

Teachers are human, too! If your child does have a dispute with a teacher, listen to what the teacher has to say. You have every right to investigate and clarify the situation, but use some tact. If you attack the teacher without listening to his or her side of the story, the teacher will lose respect for you and will like your child less, especially if you back your child at all costs and refuse to listen to the adult. Becoming defensive is simply human nature. Teachers have feelings and emotions, and if they are attacked, they will have a much more difficult time being objective with your child. Try as they may, and they may try very hard, memories will get in the way.

Try to confront the teacher in a professional manner. Calmly ask questions and listen to the answers. If you are not satisfied with the answers, don't get emotional and angry. Politely say, "Thank you for the information. Just to let you know, I will be talking to the principal." Then talk to the principal, who will (it is hoped) rectify the situation. Be an adult. If your child asks, tell them that you are handling the situation. Don't bad-mouth the teacher—see the next tip!

If after the principal has dealt with the situation and you still do not feel like it is resolved, you can take the issue to the superintendent of schools, a school board member, the entire school board, or even a state agency. You will probably have more success if you stick with the chain of command. Each level will respect you more if you try to work the situation out at each level.

TIP #3:
Refrain from Bad-mouthing Teachers

Never bad-mouth a teacher or the school in front of your child. If you don't respect the teacher or school, you are basically giving your child the right to disrespect them, too. If your child loses respect, you are in for a very long year and quite possibly a long school career. Giving your child permission to disrespect the teacher or the school will make things difficult for you in the long run. There are probably many situations in a day where a student who has permission to disrespect teachers can and will do exactly that.

Imagine the phone calls home from teachers and principals if your child is getting in behavioral tussles at school all day long. It is a law of human nature that your child has a "personal bank account" with every person they come into contact with during the day. They can make deposits by doing good, respectful things or withdrawals by being disrespectful. Children who have a large personal bank account with the people they are working with every day will have much more success and their lives will be easier.

Children respect their parents and will believe every word they say. Keep your negative feelings and words away from your child's ears so you don't set them up for failure.

TIP #4:
Parent/Teacher Conferences

At parent/teacher conferences, first seek to understand, and then to be understood. Listen, and then ask as many questions as you want about your child. Don't ask about your child's friends since that is confidential information, and it puts the teacher in an uncomfortable position. If you have a problem with the teacher, ask to schedule an individual conference with the teacher at another time.

Also, make sure you go to conferences even if you think your child is doing great. It means a lot to the child, teachers like to say good things about students, and you might find out some surprising information.

Questions to Ask at Conferences

If the teacher doesn't cover the following areas in their scripted conference with you, feel free to ask questions. That is exactly what conferences are all about.

- How does a student earn a grade in your class?
- Is work coming in on time?
- Do you have a daily homework assignment? Could you show me a sample?
- How is the quality of the work? Do you have any samples?
- Do you hand back completed work?
- How does my child do on tests and quizzes?
- How often do you test?
- Do you think my child is studying for tests?
- Do you hand out a study guide at the beginning of the chapter?
- Do you have a cumulative exam at the end of the year?
- Are there any projects due this quarter?
- How is my child's behavior in class? Have you had to reprimand him or her for anything?
- Do you see my child as having a positive or negative attitude?
- Is my child appropriate with you as far as asking questions, asking for extra credit, etc.?
- How do you think my child is doing socially? Do they seem to fit in? If not, do you have any advice?
- In general, do you see their friends as positive?
- Have you noticed any problem with sight, hearing, or attention?
- What can I do to help?
- If I need to get hold of you, how do you prefer I do it (direct call, voice mail, e-mail)?

After asking the above questions and any others you choose, it is a great idea to give the teacher a card with vital information on it about you and your child. This will make it easier for the teacher to contact you and could also help out in case of an emergency. Many students have last names that are different from their parents' names, so sharing all of this information is helpful. End the conference by making a statement similar to the following and sharing your "parent card."

"If my child starts to fall behind, his or her grades start to slip, or you have any other concerns, please call me." (Give the teacher a card.)

The card could contain the following information, plus any other information you think would help the teacher with your child's situation.

Name of student
Name(s) of parent(s)
Work numbers (including when you can be reached)
Home numbers (including when you can be reached)
Address

If your child does not have both parents at home, you may want to let the teacher know the living arrangements and preferences as to who would get the phone call if the teacher needs to contact parents.

Ideally, divorced parents are still working together for the benefit of their child so one call can be made by the teacher and information can be passed on to the other parent. Please try to avoid putting the school and teacher in the middle of any custody disputes.

Student-led Conferences

Many middle schools use a student-led format for conferences. In this format, you meet with your child's advisor and your child leads the conference. The child summarizes each class and the advisor usually speaks about how he or she is doing in their particular class. Leading the conference really forces your child to become a partner

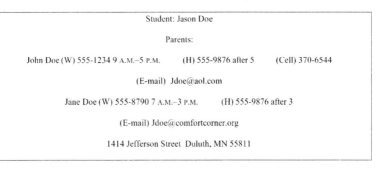

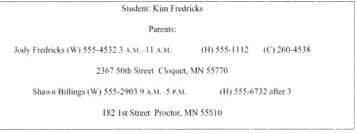

Figure 2.1.   Sample Cards

in his or her learning experience. It holds the student accountable. He or she must accept responsibility for grades and actions.

Some students will attempt to pit their parents against their teachers. This format prevents that from happening. The advisor is your first contact person at the school, so you should work hard to establish a positive relationship with this person.

While this format can be very beneficial for your child, you do not get to meet all of your child's teachers. Encourage your school to have some open conferencing times so you can at least meet each teacher and give them your card.

Chapter Three

Dealing with Other Kids

I have heard many parents say that their worst fear is that their child will end up with the "wrong crowd." As a matter of fact, it is something I have been fearful about, both when my daughter was in middle school and as my son approaches that age. Peer acceptance and rejection can be very powerful motivators for your child to act differently than you have taught. They can also lead to heartache and depression. I believe the best defense is to be proactive. Talk to your child about important issues *before* he has to address them in real life.

ISSUE #1:
"Bad Kids"

What are "bad kids" anyway? Do they beat kids up? Do they swear and spit? Do they cheat on schoolwork? Do they talk about other people behind their backs? Do they use drugs or alcohol? These questions are valid questions because everyone interprets *bad* in a different way.

If you can define what a "bad kid" is and match your child's definition of one, you can reach some common ground. This can be a scary exercise because it lays all you have taught your child on the line. You may have some disagreements that will need to be debated and ironed out, but the end product will be worthwhile.

It is important that you do not tell your child what is bad without discussion. If a child feels ownership, she will have a tougher time justifying her friendship with someone who is doing something she previously agreed to as "bad."

As a teacher, I have the belief that every child has something in them that is great. I truly believe that all of the so-called "bad kids" are just confused, sad, angry, underchallenged, scared, or simply without direction.

One of my jobs is to try to help them see the good things an education can provide and hope that they will turn their lives around. This is tough to do if the children don't have a very supportive home life. A challenging home life is not, however, an excuse for treating others poorly or for academic underachievement.

My creed that keeps me from feeling sorry for all of my emotionally/behaviorally disordered students is: For every one of these students who are taking their problems out on everyone else, there are a hundred who have the same or worse conditions at home, but they are working hard and thriving in school.

As a parent, I really would rather keep my child away from these troubled youths until he or she gets things figured out. This may sound selfish, but when it comes to our own children, I think we have to try to help them to get to adulthood with as few negative experiences as possible. Trying to keep a child away from "bad kids" may help us reach that goal.

The related worksheets in the appendix of this book (appendix, sections 2a and 2b, pages 140–41) provide an opportunity for you and your child to reach common ground about "bad kids" before a situation arises. This will allow you to be proactive instead of reactive.

After you and your child have filled out this form, have *them* look for differences. Have a discussion about differences and similarities. Reach an agreement about how to handle this issue.

ISSUE #2:
Smoking

While this may seem to be a small issue compared to the topics of drugs and alcohol, discussed below, I believe there is a very strong relationship between the two. While I have no objective evidence, I believe a student who begins to smoke cigarettes in middle school has a much greater chance of trying alcohol and drugs during that time.

My years of experience and discussions I have had with students in the past lead me to strongly believe this is true. Smoking is seen as a form of rebellion, as are drinking and drugs. Smoking carries with it a stigma that the student wants to be identified with in the view of other students; so also do drinking and drugs.

Smoking is addictive, leading the student to want to up the ante for a greater high. Everyone knows that smoking is bad for your health. Some students see smoking as a way to show that they are tough and don't worry about getting sick. A serious conversation about smoking is an important key to success in middle school.

Signing a contract with your child will help to guarantee that he or she won't make the decision to smoke lightheartedly. A pre-set consequence of the choice will also deter the decision. (See the appendix, section 3, page 142, for this contract.)

ISSUE #3:
Drugs, Alcohol, and Other Chemicals

This topic needs more than a simple "Just Say No" lecture. There is a real possibility that your child will be offered a chance to try abusing some sort of chemical in middle school/junior high, if not before then. If you just tell him that drugs are bad and he should not try them, you are risking the future of your child. At this age, parents know very little about the "real world" according to their kids.

Table 3.1.   Drugs and 8th-graders

Alcohol	80% of students have consumed alcohol (more than a few sips) by the end of high school.
Marijuana	22.0%
Inhalants	11.1%
Stimulants	7.2 %
Hallucinogens	3.4%
Prescription painkillers (Oxycotton, Lortabs . . .)	2.7%
Crack cocaine	2.1%

According to The National Institute on Drug Abuse (NIDA), the following are drugs that your 8th-grade child could have access to and the prevalence of use:

Meth

While statistics show that meth use among teens and middle-school students has been level for the past few years, experts caution that those numbers can be deceiving, since meth seems to spread in pockets, leaving some regions or populations relatively untouched while others are devastated. In school districts where I live in Minnesota, some are struggling with pockets of meth use in their schools and some remain untouched. There are pockets of meth use within certain classes. Beware of this very dangerous drug.

Alcohol: More Specifics

A child who reaches age 21 without smoking, abusing alcohol, or using drugs is virtually certain never to do so.

Joseph A. Califano Jr., chairman and president,
The National Center on Addiction and
Substance Abuse at Columbia University

According to Focus Adolescent Services, the average age when youth first try alcohol is eleven years for boys and thirteen years for girls. The average age at which Americans begin drinking regularly is 15.9 years old.

According to research by the National Institute on Alcohol Abuse and Alcoholism, adolescents who begin drinking before age fifteen are four times more likely to develop alcohol dependence than those who begin drinking at age twenty-one.

Personally, I see alcohol use as one of the biggest potential problems facing middle school parents, especially in light of the above quote. A good solid talk with your child about the risks of alcohol is a great investment. You could discuss the above facts and the prevalence of alcoholism in your family. Most medical professionals now believe that there is a hereditary factor in alcoholism.

Some parents think that if their child only drinks, that's okay. At least he isn't doing meth, smoking pot, or doing something worse. The reality of alcohol use is that it affects more people in our country in a negative way than any other drug. Some of our children may have no problem handling alcohol when they are adults. They are not equipped to handle all the negative consequences that can result from trying alcohol at a young age.

One of my biggest worries is that kids put themselves in dangerous situations while using alcohol. They may make themselves susceptible to rape, car accidents, and long-term addiction.

The best way to deal with this is to let your child know the consequences that you will give her if she uses. I have had many parents threaten their children with not getting their driver's license until they are eighteen years old.

Ask your child what he or she thinks would be a fair consequence. You may be surprised at the answer. This also gives a child some more ownership of her actions.

Marijuana: More Specifics

According to the NIDA, 22 percent of 8th-graders report having tried marijuana. There is a great misconception among teens that pot is a harmless drug. Any time I bring up the subject in my class, I find that students have readily available arguments as to why pot is okay. They say: "Pot is not addictive." "They use it to treat pain in some states, so it must not be that bad." "I know adults who smoke pot, and they have smoked their whole lives and they are fine." All of these arguments are baseless but must be dealt with if kids are going to be convinced not to try smoking marijuana.

Myth: Pot is not addictive. **Fact:** Marijuana is psychologically and physically addictive. In 2002, over 280,000 people entering drug treatment programs reported marijuana as their primary drug of abuse. If the drug was not addictive, why would so many people check themselves into a treatment program to quit?

Myth: They use it to treat pain in some states, so it must not be that bad. **Fact:** Some states have laws that allow medicinal use of marijuana. The use is legal only for patients with certain medical conditions.

Myth: I know adults who have smoked their whole lives and they are fine. **Fact:** According to the National Institute of Drug Abuse, smoking marijuana increases your chances of cancer, lung and airway problems, and of damaging your immune system.

A few years ago, I filled in for a senior high guidance counselor for the second half of the school year. Because I was only filling in, I decided to start my time in guidance by identifying ten students whose grades had taken a turn for the worse from the previous year. I found ten students in various grades who had gone from grade point averages in the 3's (Bs and As) to the 1's (mostly Ds and Fs). One by one, I called the students into my office. The results were truly amazing.

I tried to address with the students anything that may have been an important variable in their recent school struggles. Of the ten students, two had struggled with lots of physical illnesses during the current school year. Three of the students were struggling with family problems and needed some professional counseling for possible depression. One student said he was just having a bad year, but it would get better.

The remaining four students had begun to use marijuana. They all expressed that they really didn't care that much about school anymore. School seemed like a dumb waste of time to them. They were missing a lot of school, skipping classes, and failing to turn in assignments or study for tests. Their parents were concerned about their grades, but, "They couldn't figure out what was wrong with me," according to one of the students.

After this experience, I began to call pot the "great dream killer." It seems to sap the motivation out of everyone who smokes it, killing their dreams for the future.

You have to use some combination of logic, emotions, and scare tactics to get your children to understand the implications of introducing chemicals into their bodies. Simply put, the best way that you can avoid a disastrous experience with your child and chemicals is to avoid putting him or her into unsupervised situations with peers. Because alcohol and drugs effects are so different, it is almost impossible to produce a list of warning signs.

As with any potential crisis, you should always be observing your child for any changes in behavior. Dropping grades, changing clothing styles, changing friends, or loss of interest in activities that were once enjoyed are all red flags. On the other hand, I had a mother tell me that when her daughter began using meth (a senior high student), she was happier, her grades went up, and she was losing weight, something she had as a personal goal. Many drugs will seem to improve a person's life until the physical and emotional effects set in.

As an icebreaker, go to the appendix, section 4, page 143, and research the questions together and thoroughly discuss the answers.

After you have completed the drugs, alcohol, tobacco, or other chemicals worksheet, take it a step further by doing some of the possible assignments with your child.

Possible Assignments

(A) Role-play with your child:
- An older student tempts drug usage

- A group of friends at a party start drinking
- A friend starts inhaling gas, paint, or glue

(B) Call the local M.A.D.D. (Mothers Against Drunk Driving) chapter to ask if a member would meet you and your child to talk about her experience or even speak in one of your child's classes. Teachers are usually very willing to let a speaker with a great message come and speak to their class (especially the social studies or health teachers!).

(C) Ask your school if they have an S.A.D.D. (Students Against Driving Drunk) chapter in your school. Middle school/junior high students don't drive, so this is improbable. Ask if the school does anything to promote the non-use of chemicals. If D.A.R.E. is in your schools, volunteer to help with your time or money. You could also ask about having students from the high school's S.A.D.D. group come to your school to speak.

(D) Discuss anyone in your family who has struggled with any chemical addiction and discuss the fact that chemical dependency is known to be inherited.

(E) Sign a contract with your child agreeing that the child will avoid using drugs, alcohol, or any other chemical. Be open with him and ask him frequently if he has been approached. As your child gets older, you may both want to sign a contract saying he will not drive drunk or ride with anyone who is drunk or under the influence of any other chemicals. This contract guarantees that you will pick your child up anywhere/anytime and will not lecture or be angry with him/her that night, but a serious conversation will follow the next day. (See the appendix, sections 5 and 6, pages 144–45, for the drugs, alcohol, or other chemicals contracts.)

Drugs, alcohol, and other chemicals are a real part of the teenage experience. By pre-teaching and holding a constant dialogue with your child, you may be able to prevent a tragedy from occurring.

ISSUE #4:
Friends and Friendship

Many junior high/middle schools bring together many students who do not know each other. Often students have been attending different elementary schools and come together at a common junior high/ middle school. Your child will likely experience several changes in friendships during the first few years of secondary school. She will have her "old" friends from elementary school and will have the opportunity to make many "new" friends.

As a teacher, I see many very good friendships lost because students are unable to make a new friend while keeping their old friends. A good conversation about respecting everyone's feelings during this time of change would probably cut down on the amount of broken hearts.

If your child has a good set of friends going into junior high/middle school, you should encourage her to try to keep contact with them because they will probably always be there. Your child should expect a certain amount of jealousy from "old" friends as she makes new friends, but you should encourage her to listen to what they are saying.

I think many of us as adults have a great friend that we met in early elementary school, possibly even kindergarten. These friends are really irreplaceable. And parents should probably encourage keeping in contact with them. I recently had a girl who was on a team I coach transfer back to her old school. One of the reasons she gave for wanting to go back was to be with her "kindergarten friends."

I have had numerous students come to me to tell me that a friend is starting to hang around with a tough crowd and will not listen to old friends because they aren't "cool" anymore.

As most of us know, a true friend will always stick with us. This is a good litmus test to ask your child: "Is your new friend making you do anything to stay friends?" If your child says the new friend is making these kinds of demands, I would advise him or her to run like the wind. That is a sure sign that trouble is coming if it is not already at the door.

It is also a good idea to fill out a form on each friend that becomes a serious friend. I got this idea from a foster home that worked with difficult kids who usually picked poor friends. (See the appendix, section 7, page 146, for the friend form.)

This form is used not only to get to know your child's friends, but also to make him or her think about friendships. It can also be used in case of emergency.

ISSUE #5:
When Friends Fight

Sometimes even the best of friends get in disagreements with each other. Many times these differences will get worked out naturally. If there is ever a time when your child doesn't know what to do about a broken friendship, you could encourage the following steps.

Take Some Agreed-upon Time Off

Sometimes the best things friends can do for each other is to stay away. The time away may help the friends to appreciate each other more and realize how good they are for each other.

Write a Long Letter to the Friend, but Make Sure It Only Includes Positive Things about the Friendship

Most of the time the letter writing has been done by the time a parent or teacher hears about the problem, but kids are generally not good at writing reconciliation letters. Many times when kids write letters on their own, they end up being poison-pen letters. Encourage your child to keep it positive.

If the Loss of the Friendship Is Really Bothering Him, Encourage Your Child to Make an Appointment with the School Guidance Counselor

Most guidance counselors spend a decent amount of time helping to heal friendships. They may get the two friends together to broker a peace deal.

ISSUE #6:
Sex

Yes, it is a really good idea to bring up this dreaded subject before your child gets into junior high. Some students are very sexually active at this age. Even if your child is not, will not, better not . . . it is a very important issue because they may become close to someone who is sexually active.

If you have not already had the classic "birds and bees" talk with your child, it is imperative that you do it now. As with chemical use, a mixture of logic, emotions, past experiences, and scare tactics must be used to keep your child from making some sort of a huge mistake. This could be done in phases.

Phase 1

Have a heart-to-heart talk about the morality of sex before marriage. Be prepared to answer the dreaded, "Did *you* do it?" I have heard that honesty is the best policy in regard to this question, but it is an issue that is a very personal decision.

This could be a simple moral discussion based on your ethical or religious background. Try to avoid just saying it is wrong since some teenagers will take that statement as a challenge and rebel against it.

Phase 2

Have a physiological talk about how sexual intercourse can affect the body. Do some research together on sexually transmitted diseases and their long-lasting effects. Make sure you separate Phase 1 from Phase 2 so your child will understand that these are things that happen to real people. Don't assume that Phase 1 went so well that you don't need to talk about the effects on the body. This is the concrete, logical part of the discussion.

One of the best speakers ever to come to my school was a woman who spoke on abstinence. She talked for a short while about the moral issues, but she really made the students think when she talked about how pregnancy was only one physical "problem" that could come from having sex. She listed a litany of STDs and their effects, ranging from painful urination for the rest of your life, to the inability to have children, to death.

She pointed out many times that if you have sex with one person, you are sleeping with every person with whom that person has had sex during his or her whole life. Make sure you do address the issue of teen pregnancy with statistics and readings. The following information is taken from the March of Dimes.

Teenage Pregnancy

Teenage birthrates in this country have declined steadily since 1991. While this is good news, teen birthrates remain high, exceeding those in most developed countries (National Center for Health Statistics 2001). High teen birthrates are an important concern because teen mothers and their babies face increased risks to their health, and their opportunities to build a future are diminished.

- About 11 percent of all U.S. births in 2002 were to teens (ages 15 to 19). The majority of teenage births (about 67 percent) are to girls ages 18 and 19 (National Center for Health Statistics 2003).

- About 860,000 teenagers become pregnant each year, and about 425,000 give birth (National Center for Health Statistics 2003).
- About one in three teenagers becomes pregnant before age 20 (National Campaign to Prevent Teen Pregnancy 2004).
- The teenage birthrate is declining. Between 1991 and 2002, the rate fell by 30 percent (from 61.8 per 1,000 women to 43) (National Center for Health Statistics 2003). Still, in 2002 (the most recent year for which data are available), about 4 teenage girls in 100 had a baby.
- About 17 percent of teen mothers go on to have a second baby within three years after the birth of their first baby (National Center for Health Statistics 2001).
- Teen mothers are more likely than mothers over age 20 to give birth prematurely (before 37 completed weeks of pregnancy). In 2002, the 7,315 girls under age 15 who gave birth were more than twice as likely to deliver prematurely than women ages 30 to 34 (21 vs. 9 percent) (National Center for Health Statistics 2003). Babies born too soon face an increased risk of newborn health problems and even death, as well as lasting disabilities.

A Teen Mother's Health Affects Her Baby

Teens too often have poor eating habits, neglect to take their vitamins, and may smoke, drink alcohol, and take drugs, increasing the risk that their babies will be born with health problems. Studies also show that teens are less likely than older women to be of adequate pre-pregnancy weight and/or to gain an adequate amount of weight during pregnancy (twenty-five to thirty-five pounds is recommended for women of normal weight). Low weight gain increases the risk of having a low-birth-weight baby (less than five and one-half pounds).

- Pregnant teens are more likely to smoke than pregnant women over age 25. In 2002, 13.4 percent of pregnant teens ages 15 to 17 and 18.2 percent of those ages 18 to 19 smoked, compared to 11.4

percent of all pregnant women (National Center for Health Statistics 2003). Smoking doubles a woman's risk of having a low-birth-weight baby and also increases the risk of pregnancy complications, premature birth, and stillbirth.

- Pregnant teens are the least likely of all maternal age groups to get early and regular prenatal care. In 2002, 6.6 percent of mothers ages 15 to 19 years received late or no prenatal care (compared to 3.6 percent for all ages) (National Center for Health Statistics 2003).
- A teenage mother is at greater risk than women over age 20 for pregnancy complications such as premature labor, anemia, and high blood pressure. These risks are even greater for teens who are under 15 years old (National Center for Health Statistics 2003). These youngest mothers also may be more than twice as likely to die of pregnancy complications than mothers ages 20 to 24 (The National Campaign to Prevent Teen Pregnancy 2004).
- Three million teens are affected by sexually transmitted diseases annually, out of a total of 12 million cases reported. These include chlamydia (which can cause sterility), syphilis (which can cause blindness, maternal death, and death of the infant), and HIV (the virus that causes AIDS, which may be fatal to the mother and infant) (Centers for Disease Control and Prevention 2004).

Health Risks to the Baby

A baby born to a teenage mother is more at risk of certain serious problems than a baby born to an older mother.

- In 2002, 9.6 percent of mothers aged 15 to 19 years had a low-birth-weight baby (under 5.5 pounds), compared to 7.8 percent for mothers of all ages. The risk is higher for younger mothers: 11.3 percent of 15-year-old mothers had a low-birth-weight baby in 2002 (18,703 girls this age gave birth, and 2,112 had low birth-weight babies), compared to 8.9 percent of women aged nineteen (168,111 births, with 14,920 of low birth-weight) (National Center for Health Statistics 2003).

- Low-birth-weight babies may have organs that are not fully developed. This can lead to lung problems such as respiratory distress syndrome, or bleeding in the brain, vision loss, and serious intestinal problems.
- Low-birth-weight babies are more than 20 times as likely to die in their first year of life than are normal-weight babies.

Other Consequences of Teenage Pregnancy

Life often is difficult for a teenage mother and her child.

- Teen mothers are more likely to drop out of high school than girls who delay childbearing. A 1997 study showed that only 41 percent of teenagers who have children before age 18 go on to graduate from high school compared to 61 percent of teens from similar social and economic backgrounds who did not give birth until ages 20 or 21 (The National Campaign to Prevent Teen Pregnancy 2002).
- With her education cut short, a teenage mother may lack job skills, making it hard for her to find and keep a job. A teenage mother may become financially dependent on her family or on public assistance. Teen mothers are more likely to live in poverty than women who delay childbearing, and over 75 percent of all unmarried teen mothers go on welfare within five years of the birth of their first child (The National Campaign to Prevent Teen Pregnancy 2002).
- Teens may not have good parenting skills or have the social support systems to help them deal with the stress of raising an infant.
- A child born to an unmarried teenage high school dropout is 10 times as likely as other children to be living in poverty at ages 8 to 12 (Annie E. Casey Foundation 2003).

- A child born to a teenage mother is 50 percent more likely to repeat a grade in school and is more likely to perform poorly on standardized tests and drop out before finishing high school (National Campaign to Prevent Teen Pregnancy 2002).

The March of Dimes

The mission of the March of Dimes is to improve the health of babies by preventing birth defects and infant mortality. Through programs of research, community services, education, and advocacy, the March of Dimes continues its successful fight to save babies.

Because of the risks involved in teen pregnancy to both mother and child, the March of Dimes strongly urges teenage girls to delay childbearing. The March of Dimes also recommends that anyone who could become pregnant eat a healthy diet, manage her weight, and quit smoking. They further recommend that teenage girls take a multivitamin containing folic acid every day for their own health and to reduce the risk of having a baby with birth defects of the brain and spinal cord should they become pregnant.

Teens who already are pregnant can improve their chances of having a healthy baby by:

- Getting early and regular prenatal care from a health care provider or clinic.
- Eating a nutritious and balanced diet.
- Stopping smoking (and avoiding secondhand smoke). Smoking increases the risk of low birth-weight, premature birth, stillbirth, and pregnancy complications.
- Stopping drinking alcohol and/or using illicit drugs. Alcohol and drug use limits fetal growth and can cause birth defects.
- Avoiding all prescription and over-the-counter drugs (including herbal preparations), unless recommended by a health care provider who is aware of the pregnancy.

For more information about pregnancy, visit the March of Dimes Pregnancy and Newborn Health Education Center. For a catalog of education materials, brochures, information sheets, videos, and Spanish language materials, contact the March of Dimes Resource Center.

It is important to point out that *no* birth control, except abstinence, can totally protect a person from STDs or an unwanted pregnancy.

Phase 3

Talk to your child about putting themselves into risky situations.

There are situations that children can put themselves into that are dangerous. They may have made up their minds to abstain from sex, but if they go to a party and get drunk or find themselves alone with a person they do not trust, they may be risking that creed. Date rape has been found to be very common. Talk to your child about staying in groups and abstaining from influences that may cloud their judgment. Assure them that you would drop anything to get them out of a bad situation and to keep them safe.

Phase 4

Beg and plead!

ISSUE #7:
Popularity

Popularity is a huge issue for middle school/junior high students. In my opinion, the popularity phase peaks in the early part of 8th grade and slowly becomes less of an issue as students get older. Being "popular" to a teen can really matter or be a very small issue.

What is "popular," anyway? From the research I have done, it really depends on the makeup of the school the child is attending.

Some schools mark popularity by looks, some by how much money a person has, and some by a formula that no one will ever figure out.

The most important issue will be how you teach your child to handle popularity. Changing his or her personality to fit the "formula" can be damaging to an adolescent's soul. Talk openly about how popularity fades fast and is a nonfactor in the world of adults. Make sure your child realizes that many of the people that he or she might be trying to impress will not even be a part of his or her life in about five or six years.

Continually talk to your children about being themselves and surrounding themselves with people who like them for who they are, not the amount of money they have or how much time they spend getting their faces ready for school.

I have taught many students who are "popular" because they are friendly to everyone and are just positive human beings. If your child insists that you are crazy and don't understand their world, convince them that one thing is for sure. "Popular" people have a lot of confidence in themselves and other people. They make other people want to be around them because of their positive personality. If your child still thinks you are out of touch, relax, he may have to learn this lesson on his own!

ISSUE #8:
Put-downs/Teasing

This may seem like a small issue compared to some of the issues discussed above, but it can become the main focal point in an adolescent's life if not addressed. Put-downs and teasing begin before junior high/middle school, but I believe they become potentially more dangerous at the junior high/middle school age.

First of all, junior high/middle school students are growing fast, so they may be able to do actual physical damage to one another if the teasing escalates to a physical confrontation. A victim of verbal or physical bullying will suffer more in these years as they are older and probably care more about their peers' perception of them. A proactive plan about both sides of a put-down situation may be helpful.

The Bully

I talk frequently about put-downs in my classroom. I tell students that the only reason someone has to put another person down is to make him- or herself feel better. The bully attempts to shove someone down further than he is by making his victim feel bad about him- or herself. The problem is that it is an ineffective way to accomplish this goal. If the bully has a conscience (99 percent do), he will actually feel bad about the situation later. The victim surely feels bad so it is a lose-lose situation.

If your child has ever been a part of this, one of the best things to talk about is empathy (being able to put yourself in someone else's place) and the Golden Rule (Do to others what you would have them do to you). If this does not seem helpful, role-playing a situation could benefit your child.

The Victim

Most people see the victim as having two choices: fight back or run away. There is probably a time and place for each of these potential solutions, but I would like to propose a very seldom-used solution for verbal bullying. *Please, please, please have your child let somebody in his or her school know that this bullying is happening.*

Most kids who are verbally bullying are not bad kids, so an adult they respect may be able to stop the problem. Your child may be accused of tattling, but if the student is of the great majority who has a conscience, he or she will stop the verbal aggression.

Physical aggression is a different story. This is a time when you must tell the principal of the school. In most cases, the police will be called, and charges will be filed. Does this sound rather harsh? It is, and for good reason. The school district where I am employed has a zero tolerance policy for harassment of any type, as do most school districts.

A strong message must be sent to students who want to be physically violent. This message will, if taken seriously, have an effect on the way the bully will solve his or her problems or differences later in life. I know it is a cliché, but you will be doing them and everyone around them a great favor. If the physical aggression does not stop, the student may have to be removed from the school.

In reality, adolescents will normally try to take care of this problem themselves. They may not want to worry their parents or they may not want to look weak. How do you know if your child is a victim of bullying if she will not tell you? The Johnson Institute in Minneapolis has adapted a list of some common characteristics of passive and provocative victims of bullying from Dan Olweus, *Bullying at School: What We Know and What We Can Do* (Cambridge: Blackwell, 1993).

The Passive Victim:

- More anxious and insecure than students in general
- Cautious, sensitive, and quiet
- Commonly cries or withdraws when attacked
- Low self-esteem
- Often lonely at school
- Seems to prefer company of adults
- Is not aggressive and does not tease others
- Negative attitude toward violence and use of violence
- Physically weaker than peers
- Difficulty asserting self in a group
- Closer, more positive relationships with parents
- Lower than average level of problems, such as criminality, later in life

- Tends to "normalize" and no longer be a victim upon entering adulthood, although may have lower self-esteem and be more prone to depression

The Provocative Victim:

- Anxious and insecure
- Pattern of aggressive reactions (hot-tempered)
- Attempts to fight or answer back when attacked, but not effectively
- Often hyperactive, has difficulty concentrating, and acts in ways that irritate others
- May be clumsy, immature, or have irritating habits
- Behavior often evokes negative reactions from a large part of the class, not just from the bullies
- Often disliked by adults as well as peers
- May try to bully weaker students

   Go to the appendix, section 8, page 147, for the put-down worksheet. The worksheet's purpose is to provide some discussion topics about putdowns and bullying. It also takes the pressure off your child in that he or she "has" to tell you about any problems of this nature because this is part of the worksheet agreements.

   It is a good idea to sign an agreement with your child stating that he or she will tell you if he or she is being bullied. Many students will try to solve the problem themselves and end up getting hurt or going out of their way to avoid the bully. Taking the responsibility of telling out of their hands before the incident happens can relieve some stress.

   It is also a good idea to make a plan of action together so that your child feels some ownership and learns the proper ways to deal with problems instead of you "solving" it for him. See the appendix, section 9, page 148, for a bullying contract.

   The stark reality of bullying is that in almost all recent school shootings, the victims felt like they were being bullied for a large part of their lives. While this is certainly no excuse for violence, it has alerted school officials and parents to be more vigilant in dealing with bullying.

ISSUE #9:
Cyber Bullying

E-mail, chat rooms, instant messaging, personal web pages, and cell phone texting are just a few venues for a new trend in teenage life: cyber bullying. This may sound like a little thing, but in the past few years it has become a serious issue in the lives of many of my students.

Students are getting messages warning them not to show up at school—or else. Naturally, this could turn into a major emotional issue.

Some kids are very good at concealing their cyber bullying tactics and feel like they can never be caught. This allows them to go further with the harassment than they might in person because they are anonymous. I have had students complain that they are getting text from someone threatening them, stalking them, and even threatening family members. The bully simply blocks the caller I.D.

Blogging is a new trend among middle school and high school students. Sites such as Xanga, Facebook, Friendsation, and MySpace allow students to create a web page that others can see and participate in. This new media opportunity can also be very dangerous.

Under no circumstances should your child post his or her picture, full name, phone number, or address on these pages. There have been numerous media reports of teens meeting up with someone they met on one of these sites only to find out what they thought was a sixteen-year-old boy is a fifty-five-year-old pedophile.

A blog has also turned out to be a perfect place to bully. Students can say anything they want without being recognized. Again, threats are made, rumors are spread, and bullying happens.

Some tips for avoiding or minimizing cyber bullying:

Teach your child not to respond to threatening, obscene, or abusive messages of any kind. Don't *ever* give out personal information or passwords. If the e-mail or text was sent from someone at school, save it and print it if you can. Contact the phone or Internet company to inform them of the threat. Let the school and police know what is happening. Many schools have policies about threats and will get the police involved immediately. This is not an issue to take lightly. If the situation is allowed to go on for too long, it will distract children from school and cause them a lot of extra worries. Once the school or police get involved, the bully will usually stop. If he doesn't, charges will have to be pressed.

ISSUE #10:
Basic Internet Safety

This information is taken from the F.B.I. website, www.fbi.gov/privacy.htm, on children and the cyber world.

While on-line computer exploration opens a world of possibilities for children, expanding their horizons and exposing them to different cultures and ways of life, they can be exposed to dangers as they hit the road exploring the information highway.

There are individuals who attempt to sexually exploit children through the use of on-line services and the Internet. Some of these individuals gradually seduce their targets through attention, affection, kindness, and even gifts. These individuals are often willing to devote considerable amounts of time, money, and energy in this process. They listen to and empathize with the problems of children. They will be aware of the latest music, hobbies, and interests of children. These individuals attempt to gradually lower children's inhibitions by slowly introducing sexual context and content into their conversations.

There are other individuals, however, who immediately engage in sexually explicit conversation with children. Some offenders primarily

(*continued on next page*)

(*continued from previous page*)
collect and trade child-pornographic images, while others seek face-to-face meetings with children via on-line contacts. It is important for parents to understand that children can be indirectly victimized through conversation, that is, "chat," as well as the transfer of sexually explicit information and material.

Computer-sex offenders may also be evaluating children they come in contact with on-line for future face-to-face contact and direct victimization. Parents and children should remember that a computer-sex offender can be any age or sex. The person does not have to fit the caricature of a dirty, unkempt, older man wearing a raincoat in order to be someone who could harm a child.

Children, especially adolescents, are sometimes interested in and curious about sexuality and sexually explicit material. They may be moving away from the total control of parents and seeking to establish new relationships outside their family. Because they may be curious, children and adolescents sometimes use their on-line access to actively seek out such materials and individuals.

Sex offenders targeting children will use and exploit these characteristics and needs. Some adolescent children may also be attracted to and lured by on-line offenders closer to their age who, although not technically child molesters, may be dangerous. Nevertheless, they have been seduced and manipulated by a clever offender and do not fully understand or recognize the potential danger of these contacts.

This guide was prepared from actual investigations involving child victims, as well as investigations where law enforcement officers posed as children. Further information on protecting your child on-line may be found in the National Center for Missing and Exploited Children's Child Safety on the Information Highway web site and Teen Safety on the Information Highway pamphlets.

What Are Signs That Your Child Might Be at Risk On-line?

Your Child Spends Large Amounts of Time On-line, Especially at Night

Most children who fall victim to computer-sex offenders spend large amounts of time on-line, particularly in chat rooms. They may go on-line after dinner and on the weekends. They may be latchkey kids whose parents have told them to stay at home after school.

They go on-line to chat with friends, make new friends, pass time, and sometimes look for sexually explicit materials. While much of the knowledge and experience gained may be valuable, parents should consider monitoring the amount of time spent on-line.

Children on-line are at the greatest risk during the evening hours. While offenders are on-line around the clock, most work during the day and spend their evenings on-line trying to locate and lure children or seeking pornography.

You Find Pornography on Your Child's Computer

Pornography is often used in the sexual victimization of children. Sex offenders often supply their potential victims with pornography as a means of opening sexual discussions and for seduction. Child pornography may be used to show the child victim that sex between children and adults is "normal." Parents should be conscious of the fact that a child may hide the pornographic files on portable storage media. This may be especially true if the computer is used by other family members.

Your Child Receives Phone Calls from Adults You Don't Know or Is Making Calls, Sometimes Long Distance, to Numbers You Don't Recognize

While talking to a child victim on-line is a thrill for a computer-sex offender, it can be very cumbersome. Most want to talk to the children on the telephone. They often engage in "phone sex" with the children and often seek to set up an actual meeting for real sex.

While a child may be hesitant to give out his or her home phone number, the computer-sex offenders will give out theirs. With Caller ID, they can readily find out the child's phone number. Some computer-sex offenders have even obtained toll-free 800 numbers, so that their potential victims can call them without their parents finding out. Others will tell the child to call collect. Both of these methods result in the computer-sex offender being able to find out the child's phone number.

Your Child Receives Mail, Gifts, or Packages from Someone You Don't Know

As part of the seduction process, it is common for offenders to send letters, photographs, and all manner of gifts to their potential victims. Computer-sex offenders have even sent plane tickets in order for the child to travel across the country to meet them.

Your Child Turns the Computer Monitor Off or Quickly Changes the Screen on the Monitor When You Come into the Room

A child looking at pornographic images or having sexually explicit conversations does not want you to see it on the screen.

Your Child Becomes Withdrawn from the Family

Computer-sex offenders will work very hard at driving a wedge between a child and her family or at exploiting their relationship. They will accentuate any minor problems at home that the child might have. Children may also become withdrawn after sexual victimization.

Your Child Is Using an On-line Account Belonging to Someone Else

Even if you don't subscribe to an Internet service, your child may meet an offender while on-line at a friend's house or the library. Most computers come preloaded with Internet software. Computer-sex offenders will sometimes provide potential victims with a computer account for communications with them.

What Should You Do If You Suspect Your Child Is Communicating with a Sexual Predator On-line?

Consider talking openly with your child about your suspicions. Tell them about the dangers of computer-sex offenders. Review what is on your child's computer. If you don't know how, ask a friend, coworker, relative, or other knowledgeable person. Pornography or any kind of sexual communication can be a warning sign. Use the Caller ID service to determine who is calling your child. Most telephone companies that offer Caller ID also offer a service that allows you to block your number from appearing on someone else's Caller ID. Telephone companies also offer an additional service feature that rejects incoming calls that you block. This rejection feature prevents computer-sex offenders or anyone else from calling your home anonymously.

Devices can be purchased that show telephone numbers that have been dialed from your home phone. Additionally, the last number called from your home phone can be retrieved provided that the telephone is equipped with a redial feature. You will also need a telephone pager to complete this retrieval.

This is done using a numeric-display pager and another phone that is on the same line as the first phone with the redial feature. Using the two phones and the pager, a call is placed from the second phone to the pager. When the paging terminal beeps for you to enter a telephone number, you press the redial button on the first (or suspect) phone. The last number called from that phone will then be displayed on the pager.

Monitor your child's access to all types of live electronic communications (i.e., chat rooms, instant messages, Internet Relay Chat, etc.), and monitor your child's e-mail. Computer-sex offenders almost always meet potential victims via chat rooms. After meeting a child on-line, they will continue to communicate electronically often via e-mail.

Should any of the following situations arise in your household, via the Internet or on-line service, you should immediately contact your local or state law enforcement agency, the F.B.I., and the National Center for Missing and Exploited Children.

1. Your child or anyone in the household has received child pornography;
2. Your child has been sexually solicited by someone who knows that your child is under eighteen years of age;
3. Your child has received sexually explicit images from someone who knows your child is under the age of eighteen.

If one of these scenarios occurs, keep the computer turned off in order to preserve any evidence for future law enforcement use. Unless directed to do so by the law enforcement agency, you should not attempt to copy any of the images or text found on the computer.

What Can You Do to Minimize the Chances of an On-line Exploiter Victimizing Your Child?

Communicate, and talk to your child about sexual victimization and potential on-line danger.

Spend time with your child on-line. Have her teach you about her favorite on-line destinations.

Keep the computer in a common room in the house, not in your child's bedroom. It is much more difficult for a computer-sex offender to communicate with a child when the computer screen is visible to a parent or another member of the household.

Utilize parental controls provided by your service provider and/or blocking software. While parents should utilize these mechanisms, they should not totally rely on them. Electronic chat can be a great place for children to make new friends and discuss various topics of interest, but it is also prowled by computer-sex offenders. Use of chat rooms, in particular, should be heavily monitored.

Always maintain access to your child's on-line account and randomly check his or her e-mail. Be aware that your child could also be contacted through the U.S. mail. Be up-front with your child about your access and the reasons for it. Teach your child the responsible use of resources on-line. There is much more to the on-line experience than chat rooms. Find out what computer safeguards are utilized by your child's school, the public library, and at the homes of your child's friends. These are all places, outside your normal supervision, where your child could encounter an on-line predator.

Understand, even if your child was a willing participant in any form of sexual exploitation, that he or she is not at fault and is the victim. The offender always bears the complete responsibility for his or her actions.

Instruct your children:

- never to arrange a face-to-face meeting with someone they met on-line;
- never to upload (post) pictures of themselves onto the Internet or an on-line service to be viewed by people they do not personally know;
- never to give out identifying information such as their name, home address, school name, or telephone number;
- never to download pictures from an unknown source, as there is a good chance there could be sexually explicit images;
- never to respond to messages or bulletin board postings that are suggestive, obscene, belligerent, or harassing;
- that whatever they are told on-line may or may not be true.

ISSUE #11:
Gangs

One of the scariest things for a parent to think about is their child getting involved in a gang. Many gangs will start to recruit at a very young age because there is a use for young people in many of the illegal activities of gang members. My school does not have an overt gang problem, but school officials are constantly on the lookout for any signs of gang activity.

In researching this area, I found the best resource for parents is to see what gang prevention experts and local police say about dealing with children who may come into contact with gang members. The following information was taken from the Dodge City Police Department Gang Detail Gang Prevention Program:

What Is a Gang?

A gang is three or more people who come together under a common set or sign to commit criminal activity or participate in antisocial behavior.

How Do You Tell If Your Son or Daughter Is Involved in Gang Activity?

1. Major and sudden change in friends
2. The wearing of only certain colors and refusal to wear certain other colors and/or all their friends dress in the same color of clothing
3. Gang graffiti on hands (written in ink) and schoolbooks or graffiti in their bedrooms
4. Friends begin to call them by a nickname, i.e., Sleepy, Lil Loc, etc.
5. More than usual distancing from their family and siblings
6. Substance abuse (marijuana, alcohol, inhalants, cocaine)
7. Violations of the law, usually beginning with curfew or fighting violations
8. He/she comes home beaten up and will not allow you to call the police
9. Grades at school drop dramatically

If your son or daughter is exhibiting four or more of these outward signs, you need to get help at once!

What Do I Do If I Suspect That My Child Is Involved or Becoming Involved with a Gang?

1. Do not keep it a secret. Just as in substance abuse, denial of the gang problem will result in the loss of your child to the streets. Very few families have the expertise that it takes to deal with the problem. If immediate intervention is not begun, your family is in for a long, painful battle. Usually, if you get a third party involved (area mental health personnel, police department gang unit, sheriff's office, community corrections officers, or private counselors), you can intervene before the situation gets out of control.

2. Once the decision is made to get help, follow through with it. You must resolve that you are willing to do whatever it takes to help your child.

3. If all avenues are exhausted and your son or daughter is still involved with a gang, it is time to start looking for a change of living arrangements. Some families have needed to relocate, and others have sent their child to live with relatives. Getting them out of the world they have created for themselves is essential!

What Do I Teach My Son or Daughter about Staying Out of Gangs and Protecting Him- or Herself from Gang Violence?

The phrase "Just Say No" no longer works for gang resistance. You must teach your child to not only say *no,* but to dress *no,* talk *no,* walk *no,* and act *no!* Communication and dealing with situations in a timely manner will prevent most kids from becoming involved in the dangerous world of gangs. Spend time with your child.

REFERENCES

The Annie E. Casey Foundation. 2003. *2003 Kids Count Data Book Online.* Baltimore, MD, 6/11/03. www.aecf.org/kidscount/sld/databook.jsp. Accessed 7/04.

Centers for Disease Control and Prevention. 2004. *Healthy Youth: Health Topics: Sexual Behaviors*. www.cdc.gov/healthyyouth/sexualbehaviors/ index.htm. Updated 4/26/04, accessed 5/10/04.

F.B.I. website, www.fbi.gov/privacy.htm.

March of Dimes Birth Defects Foundation. 2005. www.marchofdimes .com/professionals/14332_1159.asp. Used by permission. Accessed 8/29/05. National Office: 1275 Mamaroneck Ave., White Plains, New York, 10605. 888-MODIMES (663-4637).

March of Dimes Resource Center. E-mail: publiceducation@modimes.org.

The National Campaign to Prevent Teen Pregnancy. 2002. *Not Just Another Single Issue: Teen Pregnancy's Link to Other Critical Social Issues*. Washington, D.C. www.teenpregnancy.org/resources/data/pdf/notjust.pdf.

The National Campaign to Prevent Teen Pregnancy. 2004. *Teen Pregnancy— So What?* www.teenpregnancy.org/whycare/sowhat.asp. Updated 2/04, accessed 5/11/04.

National Center for Health Statistics. 2001. *Births to Teenagers in the United States, 1940–2000*. National Vital Statistics Reports, 9/25/01. www.cdc.gov/nchs/births.htm.

National Center for Health Statistics. 2003. *Births: Final Data for 2002*. National Vital Statistics Reports, 12/17/03. www.cdc.gov/nchs/births.htm.

National Center for Missing and Exploited Children's Child Safety on the Information Highway web site. www.fbi.gov/publications/pguide/ pguidee.htm.

Olweus, Dan. *Bullying at School: What We Know and What We Can Do*. Cambridge: Blackwell, 1993.

Teen Safety on the Information Highway pamphlets. www.fbi.gov/ publications/pguide/pguidee.htm.

Chapter Four

What the Parent Can Do

TIP #1:
Talk about Why Education Is Important

Education is not the filling of a pail, but the lighting of a fire.

William Butler Yeats

One of the most persuasive (at least for middle-schoolers) demonstrations I have seen about the value of education was a simple poster. It had a picture of a young man holding his college diploma and leaning up against a brand-new sports car with a huge smile on his face. The caption read, "The REAL Value of Education." It was a powerful, simple message.

Some truly compelling statistics:

Table 4.1. U.S. Mean Annual Earnings by Education

Education	Annual Income
No High School	$25,953
High School	$34,518
Some College	$41,526
Bachelor's Degree	$63,413

Source: Money Income in the United States 2003, U.S. Department of Commerce.

Table 4.2.   Worklife Earnings

Education	Earnings (in Millions of Dollars)
Professional Degree	$4.40
Doctorate	$3.40
Master's Degree	$2.50
Bachelor's Degree	$2.10
Associate's Degree	$1.60
High School Diploma	$1.20
Less than High School Diploma	$1.00

Note: Earnings for full-time, year-round workers by educational attainment
for worklife of approximately 40 years.
Source: U.S. Census Bureau.

The above are some pretty powerful statistics relating to the importance of education to a person's future.

Another great argument that may be less persuasive for a middle-
schooler is that people who have a higher level of education are happier. They have jobs they enjoy and probably feel more challenged.
They may be less bored by their jobs because they must find solutions with their brains, which is generally not boring. And best of all,
if they hate their jobs, a higher educational level gives them better
opportunities to find more fulfilling employment.

TIP #2:
Have Preset Consequences for Unacceptable Behavior

Every parent wants to think that their child is going to excel in
school. All of us have fears that our children will fail miserably, and
it will be our fault. In chapter 1 we discuss how it would be beneficial to set up a grade contract with your child to give consequences
and rewards for good or poor grades.

In the interest of, once again, being proactive instead of reactive,
you should be prepared for some behavioral difficulties as your child
adjusts to junior high school. One of the things you can do is to fig-

ure out some consequences for negative actions and behaviors now, before the heat of the moment arrives. Consider the following possibilities:

(A) You get a call from a teacher because your child:
   • has been consistently tardy to class
   • has not been prepared for class
   • has disrupted the class, resulting in a removal from class
   • said something inappropriate to another student or a teacher
(B) You get a call from the principal because your child:
   • has been in a fight
   • has been removed from two classes in one day

These sound like things that need to be dealt with in a calm, rational way but also to be taken very seriously. You will be much more able to handle the situation if the consequence has been preset.

Go to the appendix, section 10, page 149, for a behavior contract. This worksheet can be completed with or without your child. Kids are usually really good at coming up with consequences before the behavior happens, and if they helped, they are usually less apt to fight the result of their behavior. They are also usually too hard on themselves!

TIP #3:
Get Organized ahead of Time

At parent/teacher conferences, it is astounding to me the amount of times I hear "But he told me that he was all caught up!" The parents who say this are coming to me with several incompletes on their child's report card and learning that their child is falling seriously behind in their schoolwork. This usually happens after the first grading period, when parents first realize that their child is setting him- or herself up for a tough 7th-grade year.

Daily communication about school is the key to success in this area. No, I'm not talking about the "How was school today?" daily question we ask and get the "Okay" or "Fine" response to. I am suggesting a daily tally sheet that your child is responsible for bringing home to you every day so you know exactly what was assigned in classes and if it was completed or not. True, they could still tell you they are done when they are not, but it will then be a bold-faced lie.

Make sure to put this responsibility squarely on your child's shoulders and not yours or their teacher's. Don't ask the teacher to write down their assignments every day, because the teacher has 145 other students to deal with and they still have to have time to teach.

At my school, the district provides each 6th-, 7th-, and 8th-grader a daily planner. If you are not so lucky, you can either photocopy the worksheet in this book, or go buy a daily planner in the store.

Go to the appendix, section 11, page 150, for a daily planner.

Another new development thanks to technology is something called a parent portal. Many districts have a web page where you can check your child's progress any time you want. Teachers do their grades on a computer-grading program that is part of the school's network. You can access this network and check to see if all assignments are complete.

You can only get a general understanding of your child's progress because not every teacher's grade books will be up to date the minute you are looking. You can sit with your child and ask them about certain assignments and monitor whether or not they are earning an acceptable grade.

TIP #4:
Set Aside Thirty to Sixty Minutes as Academic Time Every Single Day

Education is not received, it is achieved.

Anonymous

Some of the most successful students I have ever come across have had one thing in common. Their parents or guardians enforce a preset study time every day. The time is usually at the kitchen or dining room table, not in the child's room. This gives the impression that it is a family duty, and it also helps to avoid wasting time. If the student has no work for the day, which is highly improbable because they can always ask teachers for extra credit work, the time is still spent at the table reading a book of his or her choice.

I have come across foster homes that have found this habit to aid in the routine and help to establish school as a priority in their young adults' lives. As mentioned above, middle school teachers hear about students who say they are done with their work every day only to produce incomplete or failing grades at the end of the grading period. This "homework time" can be approached as, "You have to spend one hour working on homework. You might as well bring it home and get it done because the time will be spent increasing your reading skills if you don't have any work assigned from school."

TIP #5:
Give Your Child Opportunities to Assert His or Her Independence in a Positive Way

There are many ways that children can assert their independence without rebelling. Strangely enough, parents who try to control too much often end up going through a time when they have no control. Their child will do everything he or she can to let the parents know that he/she is the one who truly controls his/her own body and mind.

Parents can do better in this department if they choose their battles carefully. Think of ways ahead of time in which you can let your child make an important decision. You will notice that as you let them make the choices, many times you must give them some parameters and boundaries. When children are young, you could say, "Do you want to go to bed now with your teddy bear, or would you rather take your blanket?" It takes the argument out of going to bed and empowers them to make a choice about part of your decision. Some examples:

- Choosing clothes—with some loose guidelines (students should not be allowed to choose clothing with alcohol, drug, or inappropriate screen printing, or sexually risqué clothes). This keeps the child looking presentable. (A good guideline for you as a parent is to think, "Would my parents have approved?") If the child can pick out her own clothes and be happy, she at least controls what she is wearing.
- Choosing music from any title that does not have parental warnings on it
- Choosing where you will go to eat as a family
- Choosing which hour for homework after school
- Choosing chores, when appropriate
- Choosing and cooking one meal a week for the family with help
- Choosing three extracurricular activities each school year

This list could go on forever. It is important for kids to be able to feel important. I picked up the first part of the following analogy from early childhood family education classes in Proctor, Minnesota. The second part I see every day as parents struggle with how much control to maintain.

One of the best explanations I have ever heard about raising children was this: When your child is born, it is like being born into a darkened room. It is very scary and traumatic. The first thing the child starts to do is to look for the walls (boundaries) in the room. As soon as children are able to find a boundary, they feel somewhat at ease. They immediately begin to look for the next wall. If it is too close, they feel confined, and they may just sit there because they know that they can't go very far. If they cannot find any boundaries, they will go through life scared and unsure.

Other people, besides their parents, will try to set boundaries, but they will probably not love the child and they will not be as gentle in teaching those boundaries. Now here is the trick of adolescence: you must move the boundaries out at the right speed so your child has enough confidence to find a door. If you do it too slowly, a child will try to find another way out. If you go too quickly, the child will be helpless and unprepared.

Recently, my wife and I had a discussion about how often our daughter, who is fourteen, was trying to assert her independence by wanting to have complete control over things like clothing, piercings, and music. After dealing with these issues separately, I decided to give my kids a list of rules, some of which would be negotiable at sixteen, and some which would never be negotiable while our children are living in our home. This is what I came up with:

Never Negotiable:

No drinking
No drugs
No tattoos
No to most body piercings
No smoking
No music with parental warnings
No R-rated movies without parent approval
No unsupervised parties
No unsupervised overnights

Negotiable at 16:

Single car dates
Some body piercings

This list seemed to help stem the tide of debates and arguments. I'm sure that anyone reading this book heard the line, "Well, I'm not Jane's parent," at one time or another from their own parent. The reality of being a parent is not knowing if you are being too strict or too lenient. I think you have to just go with your gut and set the limits that seem right for your lifestyle.

I know one thing for sure. It was easier to say how tough I would be and what high standards I would have when my daughter was five years old. I have listened to friends and fellow teachers talk about how they will not have the problem with a child asking to wear certain clothes and making other questionable requests because they will have them trained to act a certain way by that time. I think my children are very well behaved, but they are normal and will ask to do things to see if they will be tolerated. And rest assured, when you tell them "No," they will tell you that you are the only parents who are so mean. It's all part of being a good, strong parent.

TIP #6:
Whether You Like It or Not,
Your Child Defines His Own Destiny

If you want success for your child more than he or she does, the child will know this and some students will exploit your care and concern to the hilt. I see students all the time who fall helplessly behind in their work, and the only ones who care about it are their parents. Their parents track down work from teachers, their parents check to see if they are done, their parents accuse the teachers of losing work, and their parents do their work for them while the student sits back and watches. This is a bad message to send to the child not only for the rest of his or her educational life but also for his or her working life.

Mom and dad will not be there to do these things when Johnny gets his first job. He will have to learn the hard way, getting fired or reprimanded by employer after employer until he learns the lesson that should have been taught to him at home: Take responsibility for your own actions. John Rosemond has a set of rules that I display in my classroom. They go like this:

The Rules

(1) Whether you like it or not, whether you accept it or not, you are completely responsible for the choices you make.

(2) If you make bad choices, bad things will happen—maybe not right away, but sooner or later.

(3) If you make good choices, it is considerably less likely that bad things will happen.

Unfortunately, when a parent takes the responsibility for the choices a child makes away from the child, she will have to learn these rules from someone else who will be less kind! Letting your child makes mistakes helps her to cope later in life with things that don't go her way. If she never has practice at dealing with adversity, she will struggle with it even more during adulthood.

TIP #7:
Don't Forget to Praise Your Children When They Do the Right Things

The following poem, "The Power of Positive Students," by an unknown author, sums up this point nicely.

"I got two A's," the small boy said.
His voice was filled with glee.
His father very bluntly asked,
"Why didn't you get three?"

"Mom, I've got the dishes done,"
the girl called from the door.
Her mother very calmly said,
"Did you sweep the floor?"

"I've mowed the grass," the tall boy said,
"And put the mower away."

His father asked him with a shrug,
"Did you clean off all the clay?"

The children in the house next door
Seemed happy and content.
The same things happened over there,
But this is how it went:

"I got two A's," the small boy said.
His voice was filled with glee.
His father proudly said, "That's great;
I'm glad you belong to me."

"Mom, I've got the dishes done,"
the girl called from the door.
Her mother smiled and softly said,
"Each day I love you more."

"I've mowed the grass," the tall boy said,
"And put the mower away."
His father answered with much joy,
"You've made my happy day."

Children deserve a little praise
for tasks they're asked to do.
If they're to lead a happy life
So much depends on you.

It is so easy to forget to praise your child. Praise, as long as it is genuine, is one of the best things you can do for your child. Many behaviorists think that it is much more powerful to praise a good behavior than to wait for bad behavior and punish. Be very careful to praise only things that deserve praise. Children pick up on fake praise immediately and it does not have a positive effect on them. Real praise should be saved for when you are truly proud of something your child has done.

Chapter Five

Parents Helping Parents

A few years ago, I was at a strategic planning meeting for our school district. The speaker was a person who traveled from district to district all over the United States to help plan for the future. As a part of his presentation, he had people get into small groups and talk about what the district's most pressing needs were.

Student test scores, facilities, and transportation costs were a few issues that were brought up. One area quickly made its way to the top. Alcohol and drug use was and still is a major concern in our community.

When the speaker reviewed the top concerns, he asked everyone to close their eyes for a minute. He then asked everyone to raise their hand if they thought that drug and alcohol use was worse in their community than in other communities. When he told people to open their eyes, we were all amazed that most hands were up. He said he had done the same thing in over fifty districts and the result was the same.

He did this to demonstrate two things: First, our district was no different than other districts—everyone thinks they have a real problem in their district. Second, that there is a problem with alcohol and drugs everywhere. All school districts need to deal with this problem.

I'm sure that your district is no different. As a parent, you may have leadership that is dealing with the problem as effectively as possible. The truth is, however, that the school district has a fairly limited effect on the problem. They can make sure the school is drug- and alcohol-free by doing locker checks and even bringing in drug-sniffing dogs. They can be on the lookout for students who are under the influence and give them consequences for their poor choices.

But all students go home! This issue really lies in the community and the community of parents. Parents generally don't become a community unless someone organizes them. They will have their groups of friends who will look out for each other's kids. But even if you have a close friend, it is not easy to let them know you heard something bad about their child.

In my school district I started a group called Looking UPP. The UPP stands for Uniting Proctor Parents. The middle school and high school principals thought up the catchy name. This is a community of parents who have banded together to make sure that we are not ignorant of our children's actions when we are not with them.

The program consists of three lists that parents can get their names on:

Parent Network—Parents place their names on a list that is available to all parents on the list. Being on that list means you want to hear from other parents about anything good or bad regarding your children. It is a way to communicate things that parents may hear in a helpful way to other concerned parents.

Safehouse List—This is a list of parents who pledge that if there is a gathering at their house it will be supervised and it will be drug- and alcohol-free. Parents on this list welcome phone calls from other parents making sure the party will be supervised.

School Supervision List—This is a list for parents who are willing to increase supervision at school activities. They do not confront behavior. They just report out of the ordinary behavior to school personnel, who confront the behavior.

Most school districts do surveys of their students about drug and alcohol use. Most schools, even schools that have the worst drug problems, have a majority of students who do not use drugs. You can use those surveys to convince your child that it is not the "normal" thing to do.

I truly believe that 98 percent of all parents want their children to be drug- and alcohol-free. If the perception of "everyone does it" bothers you as a parent, you can do something about it by starting a group like this in your school.

If students truly believe that *everyone does it*, it will be much easier for them to start. If you can re-educate the children in your district that *most students don't do it* and support them through increased communication, your community will flourish.

Starting a group like Looking UPP has many other benefits. Any time you increase communication between parents, good things happen. Sometimes it is just helpful to call a fellow parent to have a discussion about clothing styles or music. If you can say to your child that you are not the only parent who does not allow the child to listen to music with parental warnings, it is a much easier argument.

We meet once a month in the school auditorium to refresh the list, add any parents who want to join, and get educated about lots of different issues. We have had the Proctor chief of police do a presentation of the different drugs that our children could find available to them very easily, even at school. We had a recovering meth addict speak to us about his life and how to keep our children safe from meth.

After one of these meetings, I had a parent in the group approach me and say that he thought that the education part of this group was helpful, but the most valuable part of our group was the large crowd of parents standing around talking to each other a full hour after the meeting was over. I wholeheartedly agree!

Our group has a script to read to another parent so emotions do not run high. It is to be a very factual conversation between two adults that goes something like this: Hello, my name is _____, and I am a member of Looking UPP like you. I just wanted to call and let you know that I heard your daughter/son was involved with a group that was _____ (what happened) on _____ (date). You may want to talk to them about it. Thanks. Goodbye.

Our group is starting an on-line forum for parents to check out for sharing issues and ideas that have worked for them and their parenting style. This forum is purposely anonymous so parents can feel free to give their real opinions about issues. No names are used, just situations like, "What time is reasonable for a curfew for a 7th-grader on the weekend? My child tells me that none of his friends has to be in before midnight." The responses are very interesting. Most parents say that their child tries to use that one on them, too.

We also have a confidentiality agreement that each person in the group signs to protect everyone.

I believe just hearing that you are involved in a parent group like this may make your child a little more nervous about doing something that they know is wrong. Parents banding together to provide support for their children fits right in with the age-old theory that "It takes a village to raise a child." In this age of splintered community, sometimes we have to invent our own village.

Chapter Six

Suicide and Other Tough Stuff

Why devote an entire chapter to the subject of suicide and other tough stuff? It is the ultimate breakdown in communication that causes suicide, eating disorders, self-cutting, and many other adolescent difficulties.

ISSUE #1:
Suicide

Suicide is one of the topics that people would like to avoid talking about, especially when you are discussing adolescent suicide. It is one of the things in life that is incomprehensible. Why would someone who has his or her whole life ahead of them even think about ending it? There are many reasons, ranging from a relationship breakup to mental illness.

The bottom line is that suicide is an option for anyone. Statistics from the Center for Disease Control show that suicide has been increasing as an option for youths aged fifteen to nineteen. There is a noticeable difference for boys. In 1950, 3.5 boys per 100,000 committed suicide. By 1990 that number had risen dramatically to 18.1. For girls in 1950, 1.8 per 100,000 committed suicide. The number had doubled by 1990 and was 3.7. From 1980 to 1992, the rate increased among persons aged 15–19 years by 28.3 percent (from 8.5

to 10.9) *and among persons aged 10–14 years by 120 percent* (from 0.8 to 1.7). So as you can see, we have developed a trend.

Obviously, if we can provide a stable home life, keep communications open, and be observant of our child's behavior, we can decrease the risks of suicide. It is often, however, much more complicated than that. Depression is found in many adolescents. Untreated depression can definitely lead to suicide. Most parents who lose a child to a suicide were not aware of their child's intentions.

In this chapter, I go over some signs that show whether or not your child is at risk for suicide and what to do if you suspect a suicide attempt.

Emotional Signs

- depression
- hopelessness
- despair
- feeling that there are no alternatives
- guilt
- helplessness

Behavioral Signs

- changes in eating or sleeping patterns
- withdrawal from family and friends
- mood swings
- talking about suicide
- giving away valued possessions

If your child is exhibiting any of the above signs, take it seriously. Do not assume that she is joking or just looking for attention. It could be a fatal assumption. Take the mystique out of it right away by asking the straightforward question, "Are you considering suicide?"

At any rate, if you suspect that your child is planning to hurt himself, seek professional help immediately. Do not hesitate or try to solve the problem "as a family." Professionals handle these issues every day and are trained to deal with emotional situations.

If your child comes home with information that one of his/her classmates is suicidal, report it to the school counselor immediately. Counselors are trained to deal with this information and may know the child and the circumstances behind the struggle. This is not a secret that can or should be kept. You will be saving your child from a very traumatic experience by passing this critical information on to someone who knows what to do with it.

If your child keeps the secret and the friend commits suicide, your child will have to live with that for the rest of his/her life. Even though it may frighten you, I'm sure that you would want another parent to report if your child was contemplating suicide. As I tell my students who have broken a promise of secrecy, "You would rather have a friend who temporarily or permanently hates you than a dead friend."

If a suicide is completed at your child's school, pay close attention to your child and his/her friends. Suicides have been shown to "cluster" in a school or in an area. Most schools have a plan of action if this terrible tragedy occurs.

You can talk to your school about starting a Friend for Life Program, where friends promise through a written contract to report their friends if they are contemplating suicide. Go to the appendix, section 12, page 151, for a Friend for Life contract. If your child's school has the antiquated idea that if you talk about suicide, it is more likely to happen, talk to the parents of your child's friends and together start a Friend for Life group on your own.

Once again, if this issue is discussed before the heat of the moment, the solution will be at hand much more easily. Discuss the issue of suicide with your child openly and honestly. There is a fallacy that if you talk to your child about suicide, it will become an option for him/her. More importantly, if you don't talk, you could lose him/her forever. As a way to keep the lines of communication open, sign a contract with your child agreeing to report his/her own feelings of suicide or those of any of his/her friends. Go to the appendix, section 13, page 152, for this contract.

ISSUE #2:
Eating Disorders

Eating disorders also require great communication between you, your child, and other adults. Anorexia and bulimia affect nearly 10 million women and 1 million men, mostly young adults, and can be life threatening. Many times people other than the parents will notice some irregularities in eating habits or loss of weight. There are two main types of eating disorders.

Anorexia nervosa occurs when a person systematically reduces calories to lose great amounts of weight. In effect, anorectics starve themselves. They go for long periods of time without eating. They become fixated on more weight loss, even when they are grossly underweight.

Many times the person who suffers from anorexia is a high achiever in school and can be seen as a perfectionist. Gone unchecked, anorexia can do permanent damage to the body and can even be fatal.

Bulimia nervosa occurs when a person eats a great amount of food, then forces the removal of food from the body by vomiting, overexercising, or by using laxatives. This cycle of binging and purging can also lead to long-term and short-term detrimental effects on the body, including dehydration, damaging the tissue in the lining of the throat, tooth damage, and damage to the vital organs.

As a coach, I have had several of my athletes struggle with eating disorders. Many times, their friends will tell me to watch them eat while we are on away trips. Friends will also bring the athlete to me to admit that he or she is scared.

When I have contacted parents, the first reaction is almost always denial. If a coach or teacher calls you to tell you they are worried about your child, please listen to them. They really have no reason to make anything up. Take it as a good cue to talk to your child to get them help.

The earlier an eating disorder is dealt with, the more manageable the problem is. Schedule an appointment with a family physician and get a referral to a therapist who has dealt with eating disorders before.

Eating disorders are not logical. It is not advisable to deal with this problem on your own, since you could be wasting valuable time that could be used to treat the disorder. It will probably not be possible to talk your child out of eating abnormally and it will surely not help to try to give consequences for it. Get the help you need by seeing your family doctor.

ISSUE #3:
Self-injury

While this may seem like a strange thing to address in this book, it is a problem that has increased in occurrence in the past five years of my teaching. I have had several students who cut themselves on a regular basis. From all of the research I have done the past few years, I have found out that most mental health professionals do not have a great handle on why some adolescents, usually girls, cut themselves.

What they do know is that it is not usually a suicide attempt. The cutting is usually shallow, just enough to draw blood. Many of the students who cut have said that they have a hard time expressing themselves, and that it is a release of their stress. Most teens, after they cut, will regret they did it and try to hide it by wearing a sweat-wristband, or several of the new rubber wristbands that Lance Armstrong has made popular.

If you discover your child is injuring himself, the first step is to accept your child's feelings while letting him know you do not approve of his actions. There is a reason for the behavior that you will probably need to see a mental health professional to uncover. In order for your child to move on, this behavior must be dealt with in a loving, yet firm, manner.

As with all of the topics of this chapter, you may want to have a discussion with your child about what to do if friends come to him or her with any signs or symptoms. Explain to your child that the friend may want to keep something a secret, but there are some secrets that cannot be kept. If the friend declares an intention to hurt himself, or says that someone else is hurting him, or that he is going to hurt someone else, your child must tell a trusted adult, preferably you.

Most of the time when one of my students is struggling with an eating disorder, self-injury, or even suicidal thoughts, he or she will ask a friend to talk to me about it. The friend is put under a great deal of burden and is often scared. The friend needs some help understanding what is happening, too.

Students do not have the training or the experience to handle these problems and need to turn them over to someone who can help or find the right kind of help. The troubled friend may be mad at the reporting student, but at least he or she will be alive and getting help with a problem that no one should have to live with every day. As I tell my students, "An angry friend is better than a hurting friend or even a dead friend."

ISSUE #4:
Sexuality

This is a topic that many parents have to deal with in junior high/middle school. Middle school is a time of trying to figure out who you are. Who do you want to become? It is a time of big life questions. For some students, they start to question their sexuality.

They may have confusing feelings of being attracted to someone of the same sex. Most parents of gay or lesbian children report the first conversations and/or conflict as being in middle school. They also say that they had suspected something since the child was very young. Without addressing the moral implications of this topic, my advice is to deal with this issue in a loving, accepting, and open way. I have seen real walls of hatred built up between parents and child when they refuse to discuss this issue. Communication can lead to an environment that allows the sorting out of feelings and acceptance of those feelings.

Whatever you do, please do not close yourself off or use the word *disown* with your child. Talk with your child and try to understand how he or she feels.

Chapter Seven

Once School Starts . . .

TIP #1:
Establish a Routine

Make sure your child knows that the rules change once the school year begins. Every year I am amazed at the bedtimes my students claim. These may be exaggerated, but many students do not have a required bedtime. As a parent, it is your job to determine a reasonable bedtime. Children in this age category should get between eight and ten hours of sleep. As a parent, I know this is easier said than done.

My daughter loves to stay up late in her room. Once school starts, we hold to her bedtime of 10:00 P.M. That gives her about eight hours of sleep. Ten might be better, but I don't think we could make her go to bed at 8:00 P.M. A solid bedtime sets up the routine for the next day.

In the morning, establish a wake-up routine. Personally, I like to hit the "snooze" button once before I wake up. I think my mom, who would call for me once and then call again about ten minutes later, taught this behavior to me.

I strongly believe that a middle school student's parents are responsible for waking their child up. These children need to remain children in some ways, and the wake-up call and providing something to eat each morning are a way of showing that you have some responsibility for your child. Planning your morning and making sure it is as non-stressful as possible can start your child off on the right foot.

TIP #2:
Ask Lots of Questions of the School and Your Child

School

Don't be afraid of calling the school for any questions you may have. You have heard the saying when you were in school, "There is no such thing as a stupid question." Most schools have one or two secretaries who are there to answer questions. If the secretary doesn't know the answer, ask them to refer you to a principal, assistant principal, or guidance counselor. Communication prevents many small problems from turning into big problems and misunderstandings.

Child

If you want to be helpful to your child, you can begin by being interested. You may get the impression that he doesn't want to talk about school, but there will be days when he will. If, during the school year, you have a great talk about school five times when you asked about school 180 times, it was worth it.

Recently, I was at the eye doctor for a checkup. While I was waiting to see my doctor, I witnessed a technician having an exchange with a middle school–aged kid and his mom. The boy needed new glasses. The technician and the mom were asking him a series of questions that made me chuckle. The exchange looked something like this:

Mom: "Do you like these glasses?"

Boy: "No."

Mom: "Why not?

Boy: "I don't know. I just don't."

The mother then proceeded to go through this process with about ten pairs of glasses. The boy never left his seat. His mom went across the room each time with a new pair of glasses. Finally, she asked him why he didn't like any of the glasses she had picked out. He said "Mom, I like my old glasses." His old glasses looked like they had been through some very tough times. They were bent and worn. His mom, after a few more minutes, was able to convince the boy that he needed new glasses and picked out a pair that he could stomach. Now it was the technician's turn to speak middleschoolese. I watched as the middle-aged man, who obviously had not dealt with many teenagers, tried to size the new glasses. It was like watching a verbal wrestling match. The boy would only answer yes and no. He provided no explanation why the glasses "didn't feel right." The technician bent the frames this way and that way to fit the boy's head until the new glasses looked an awful lot like his old glasses, all bent and worn. After the mom and boy left, the technician told a fellow employee that he was sure glad he never had to deal with kids that age. "That kid drove me nuts. I wanted to shake him!" said the technician.

Both the mom and technician assumed that communication with a middle school–aged child is a two-way street. It is not, unless you know the proper ingredients. The success rate is still rather limited, but here are some tips:

If you want to establish a proper climate for talking, do not ask closed-ended questions. Closed-ended questions can be answered with a yes or a no. "Did you have a good day at school?" "Yes." "Is everything going okay at school?" "Yes." The intermediate step is to ask a question that calls for an answer other than a yes or a no. Eleven-, twelve-, and thirteen-year-olds are notorious for being able to give the shortest answer to a seemingly complicated question. "How was your day at school?" "Fine."

The best approach for getting your child to talk is to make a statement like, "Tell me about your day," or, "What are you studying in your social studies class?" This forces them to explain something to get off the hook. Again, if this technique only bears fruit a few times, it could still yield more than if you didn't ask or asked incorrectly.

It is also important to demand a child's undivided attention while you are trying to talk. For some reason, kids this age will try to distract themselves with the TV or a radio when the topic is them or their day.

TIP #3:
Volunteer

Another way to help your child's school is to volunteer. Schools can always use help. There is a high correlation between a child's success level and their parents' involvement in school. If your child is self-conscious and prefers other students not to know you are around, help with something behind the scenes. You will get to know the faculty and staff of the school much better, and they will appreciate your help.

My school has a Parents Plus group, which plans activities for the students every month. They also coordinate volunteer work with the school. We also have the parent support group called Looking UPP.

My son's elementary school has a Parent Involvement Committee, which tries to find ways to involve parents in their children's school life. Each teacher is assigned a parent who coordinates volunteers for classroom activities and projects. The bottom line is, the more you are involved in your child's school, the better chance your child has for success.

TIP #4:
Keep Communication Lines Open with Your Child by Alternating Communication Techniques

It is amazing to me how often I hear parents say, "We used to talk all the time. Now it is like pulling teeth." I have asked parents who are still communicating regularly with their child what they did that seemed to work.

Among the suggestions:

Have a Meal as a Family Every Day

This is probably the most common answer to the communication question. Parents also are advised to leave the stereo and TV off during this time. Set it up as a time when your family can talk (not argue) about things that are going on in their lives. Many families use a system to make sure everyone gets a chance.

Keep a Family Journal

This is an area where anyone in the family gets to write down problems they are having with the family or in other parts of their lives. Parents could set up a reward system for using the journal. Even if it is underused, your child will know it is there in case they need it.

Make a Date with "One Child Only" Once a Week or Once a Month

This can be with mom or dad but probably not both. Take them out to a nice restaurant and go see a movie. If you start this young, it won't seem as strange as they get older. It provides another avenue to talk about things.

Tuck Your Child In

Again, this may seem really babyish, but it may provide a time when things can be talked about. A simple, "How are things going at school for you these days?" can open up a great conversation about many topics. In my experience, the time right before bed seems to be an easier time to talk with no distractions.

All of the above recommendations will provide the opportunity for communication. More importantly, your child will get the message that the lines are open and can be used anytime.

Chapter Eight

Improving Study and Testing Skills

When a student enters a middle/junior high school one thing is always true. His or her study and testing skills will be challenged. Most elementary schools use the single teacher model, with some limited switching of teachers throughout the day. Middle/junior high school usually involves six to eight classes a day with a different subject and teacher in each class. Students need to learn to manage all of these classes and how to juggle the expectations of each teacher.

I teach a study skills unit in my 8th-grade class. Surprisingly, I find that most students do not have a system for studying. They know very few of the "tricks" to help them to remember everyday classroom materials. They struggle at taking notes in class and have no real method to study for tests.

In this chapter, I hope to give you as the parent some great ideas to help your child work smarter so he or she can learn more deeply and get better grades.

ATTITUDE

A positive mental attitude is crucial to success in school. Every math teacher's least favorite statement for a parent to mutter is, "I told my son/daughter that I was never good at math either." Telling your child that it is okay to struggle in a subject area is not a bad thing, but you have to make sure that you don't give him or her permission to quit trying or be satisfied with sub-par work.

If a child believes that she is bad at something, that very thought leads her to be bad. This is called the Pygmalion effect or the self-fulfilling prophecy. Believing you are bad at something leads to all kinds of negative behaviors like giving up quickly, turning in poor quality work, and not even trying to study for a test because you are convinced that you cannot understand the material, no matter how hard you try. When a child struggles, it is really the perfect time to teach the life lessons of persistence and resilience. Learning this lesson can pay big dividends later in life.

LAZINESS

Laziness is resting before you are tired.

Chinese proverb

I constantly harp on my students that they should never allow themselves to be lazy. There is no arena of life in which laziness is rewarded. Tell your child to take notes every time the teacher begins to give them. Encourage your child to do all the extra credit available and ask the teacher if there is anything else to do to help his or her grade.

Every quarter, I give my students an extra credit opportunity. It really impresses me when a student will do extra credit even though he or she is very confident that they have already earned an "A." Conversely, I am not impressed when a student who is a few points away from a higher grade decides not to do the extra credit so he can sit and stare into space, resting before he is tired.

BEING PREPARED FOR CLASS

For a teacher, a student who is not prepared is very frustrating. I, as do most teachers, expect students to come to class with a writing utensil, textbook, and a notebook. Different teachers will require extra materials like a bellwork journal, a calculator, or anything else needed for the specific class. From a teacher's standpoint, the student who comes in to class with just a body and nothing else gives the message that he doesn't care about learning. This is the student who disrupts the class, asking other students to borrow a pencil or a piece of paper. Forgetting something now and then is normal and classmates have no problem lending a pen to someone once in a while. But even thirteen-year-old students know when they are being taken advantage of, and they will put a stop to it by refusing to lend the item even though they may have several extras.

HOME STUDYING ENVIRONMENT

When I ask students where they study at home, I get many varying answers. The kitchen table, the living room, and other shared areas of the home are the most common answers. These places also have the most people, the most noise, and the most distractions.

Most students do not have a consistent place to study in their homes. I believe that this is very important. The perfect environment would be somewhere that is well lit, has a supply of fresh, cool air, and is free from distractions. For many students, this is their bedroom.

They should avoid listening to loud music, watching TV, or talking on the phone. Students today will try to convince you that they can multitask. Don't buy it! The human brain does not work as effectively when it is asked to do more than one thing, especially when it involves learning and memory.

It is a great idea to have a wall calendar at home so students can write due dates of projects and big assignments and tests. Just like adults, middle school kids tend to put assignments off until the last minute. Getting asked to run to Target on Sunday night for some materials for a project or presentation that is due on Monday happens less commonly when you know about it ahead of time. It's still your child's responsibility, but a reminder or two from you to get started could help him to develop the habit of working on things earlier rather than later.

EVERYDAY ASSIGNMENTS

SQ3R

This studying technique was taught to me in my freshman year of college. How I wished I had known about it sooner! The technique is based on brain research. The five steps are:

Survey—Look over the material quickly, taking note of bold print or italicized words, pictures, captions, or anything else that stands out in the chapter/reading. This step is designed to "set the table" and get your brain to recognize things when you begin reading the material.

Question—As you look over the chapter a second time, this time ask yourself questions about the reading. Go to the back of the reading and read the questions the author has written. You don't need to know the answers. Again, you are just placing some information in your brain.

The above two steps should take about five minutes, but they are the most effective five minutes you can spend.

Read—Simply read the material from beginning to end. As you read the material, things that you came across when you surveyed and questioned that material will stand out.

Recite—Close the book. To yourself or out loud, cover the material you just read from beginning to end. Recite the most important facts and concepts. Many students find telling this information to someone else or writing it down helps them to remember even more.

Review—Open the book. Again go over the material to see what you remembered and more importantly, what you missed. After you finish this step, close the book again to see if you can remember everything.

This technique works! When you first try it, it may take a little longer, but the payback of remembering more of what you read is worth the time. You will have to spend less time studying for a test because you will already know the material. After you use SQ3R for a while, you will actually cut down on the time spent reading, because you become more efficient.

PREPARING FOR A TEST

Before the Test

If your child is using SQ3R, this step will be much easier. He or she will actually know most of the material, having learned it the right way. Here are some other great tips for studying for a test:

Use mnemonic devices to remember lists and other things that need to be memorized. Mnemonic devices are memory tools, like making sentences out of the first letter of every word in a list. Let's say your child had to memorize the great lakes in order from West to East. They could make up the sentence Sam Made Harry Eat Octopus for the lakes Superior, Michigan, Huron, Erie, and Ontario. If they had to memorize the first ten presidents, they could make up the sentence Washington And Jefferson Made Monroe And Jackson Vow Hatred Toward Polk for Washington, Adams, Jefferson, Madison, Adams (Quincy), Jackson, Van Buren, Harrison, Tyler, and Polk. There are lots of other ways to use these devices, and spending time with your child making them up can actually be kind of fun.

One of the best techniques for studying that I discovered in college was to sleep on it. One of my professors noticed that I didn't do a great job on a test and that I looked quite tired the morning of the test. One of the methods I was using to try to survive college was cramming. I was staying up half the night trying to cram information into my head by repetition. This technique, used by many college students and handed down as a way to learn, does not work. The professor showed me the results of a study that clearly proved cramming made students score lower on tests than getting a good night's sleep.

He suggested studying for thirty minutes right before I went to sleep. His theory and the theory of many others was that your brain continues to work on the material you were just studying. In effect, you get some free study time while you are sleeping. If you get lucky, you might even dream about the history chapters you are being tested on!

The next step in this very effective process is to study for thirty minutes as soon as you wake up. Recalling the information right away has a way of cementing the information in your brain. It also gives you a good measuring stick as to how much more time you need to spend studying before the test begins.

Once I started to use this technique, I was much more confident, my mind was sharper, and I did a better job on tests for the rest of my college career. Once again, I wish I had known about this in junior high and high school.

During the Testing Session

The key here is to reduce test anxiety by having a plan for the test. While the teacher is getting organized and handing out the test, it is not a bad idea to review the notes or study guide one last time. Do this with confidence, knowing that the last review might come in handy later in the test. Review the material, but don't quiz yourself. Quizzing yourself and not knowing every answer could start a bout of test anxiety and panic. Just review the material to put it in your brain one last time.

After the test is handed out, take thirty seconds to relax. Breathe deeply and tell yourself that you are prepared for this test. Assure yourself that you put the work in and the payoff will be a good grade.

When you start the test, answer the questions you know without having to think much right away and skip the questions you are not immediately sure of. After answering all of the easy questions, go back to the questions that require some thought. Tell yourself, these are the questions I studied so hard to be able to answer. Answer all of these questions except for any that you truly feel you don't know. Last, guess on the remaining questions, assuring yourself that these guesses are educated guesses. Many times the brain will come up with the correct answer because you came across it in your studying.

Some Tips on Different Types of Questions

Essay

This is a description of how to write an essay that I use in my classroom: How to write an essay—five paragraphs!

Introduction Your introduction is like a map at the entrance of a museum. It gives readers an idea of where they are, where you are going to take them, and what they will see along the way.

As you think about your introduction, ask yourself:

What is my main idea or thesis?
Who are my readers?
Why is my idea important?

Body The body of the essay moves the reader along toward the destination or goal. It might have one paragraph, but usually it has more. Each paragraph is related to one of the points you want to express to readers along the way. Some points may take more than one paragraph to develop completely.

As you think about the body of your paper, ask yourself:

What points do I want to make to help my readers understand my idea?
What examples and evidence can I use to help the reader understand each point?
How can I keep the reader interested?

Conclusion   The conclusion is the end of the essay. It looks back on the points you have shown the reader, and reinforces the main idea. It also should create a feeling of ending, a goodbye to the reader.

As you think about your conclusion, ask yourself:

Has the reader's mind been changed by following my points and examples?

Keep in mind: The more you write in an essay, the better, within reason. You have a better chance to cover the material the teacher is looking for when you write more, but you must make sure that what you are writing remains meaningful.

Other Tests

Multiple choice—Use the process of elimination on tough questions. Eliminate the choices that are obviously wrong to narrow down good choices.

Matching—Fill in the easy ones first so your tough choices are limited to a few. Most of the time this process leaves questions where common sense can be used to plug in the remaining answers effectively.

True and false—Again, skip over the hard questions and come back to them later. Most of the time, when the words *never* or *always* are used, the answer is false. You have a 50/50 chance, so relax!

Short answer—Write as much as you can fit in the space provided.

Fill in the blank—These questions you either know or you don't.

For all types of questions, if you have studied, you can have some confidence in the ones you have to guess on. *Do not leave any answers blank.*

If your child has true test anxiety, recognize it as a serious problem to learn about and overcome. In some cases, accommodations can be made so the child has a greater chance for success. Some accommodations could include having the test read to them, answering orally, or going to a room by themselves to take the test. In my opinion, these techniques can be used temporarily, but the anxiety should be dealt with by teaching relaxation techniques and other coping strategies to the child. Sometimes I think that making accommodations just extends the problem into the high school and college years, making those times more difficult.

INSTILL PRIDE FOR DOING GOOD WORK

Everyone remembers the kid in school who would tease the good students for caring about school. He would call them nerds or geeks and he had plenty of supporters. This kid is still in school! It is probably the son or daughter of the one you remember. Sometimes this kid can make it difficult to be a strong student. It is your job to instill that pride in doing great work. One way to do this is by explaining that the student who is putting others down will probably be working for them some day, making a whole lot less money and being far less satisfied with his job.

Doing great work in school has many rewards. Being more intelligent, scoring higher on the SAT and ACT tests, having more college choices, and earning scholarships are just a few of these rewards. All of these things are examples of delayed gratification, which is a great concept for a person to learn.

Chapter Nine

Advice to an 8th-grader

Every year in May, for a day I get to visit the seniors I taught five years before. It is one of my favorite days of the year. I do lots of activities with them, including giving them a letter that they wrote to themselves when they were in 8th grade. I also have them fill out a sheet of paper called "Advice to an 8th-grader."

I tell the seniors that they just lived through the 9th through 12th grades. What do they wish someone had told them so they could have avoided mistakes during those years? I ask them about alcohol and drugs, friends, boys/girls, school, parents, extracurricular activities, teachers, and one thing they would have changed about their middle school and high school experience.

I tell the seniors to pretend that they are talking to a younger brother or sister and to be honest. I do not want them to write their names. The only other rule I have is that they do not swear on the paper.

Every year, throughout the year, I read them to my 8th-grade classes. I tell my middle school students that we will read all of the responses, not just the good ones. I can do this with confidence because I know the good ones outweigh the bad ones by 75 to 1. I try to point out that there are trends in all of the advice given. I also tell them to envision how successful a person is if they are talking about getting drunk often and experimenting with drugs.

The other thing that I point out to my students is that some students will offer the advice to "try alcohol, but just don't get hooked." For many people, this is sufficient advice, but for about 20 percent of the population, this is not great advice. This 20 percent is composed of students who will become chemically dependent. In my opinion, their life, as far as chemicals are concerned, is predetermined. They will become increasingly dependent until the only thing that matters is the next time they can drink. Their grades and relationships with their family and friends will deteriorate. If they do not get help, they will struggle with this dependence for the rest of their lives.

If my students have close relatives who, they think, may have a drinking problem, I tell them that the odds of the students being in the 20 percent at risk are very high. They should never start drinking, especially in middle or high school.

There is also evidence that the earlier a person starts to drink alcohol, the higher the chance that they will become chemically dependent.

Here are some examples of "Advice to an 8th-grader." If you want to use this activity with your child, make sure you emphasize that these are taken from *real* seniors in high school. These tips can generate great discussions.

ALCOHOL AND DRUGS

Learn to deal with alcohol and drugs in a responsible way. Try it, but only if you want to—not because other people want you to.

According to my experience, I advise you not to take any drug, and if you decide to take drugs, think of the effects of the drug. It can destroy your life.

Don't be in hurry to try it. The younger you are, the easier it is to just sink in it. Drugs are—don't ask, but it's really bad.

My advice on alcohol is don't make it your life. My advice on drugs is to just stay away from it; it can ruin your life.

It's unrealistic to tell you not to try alcohol and drugs because it's natural to be curious about them. But be careful and don't get hooked—it's not cool to have to leave school at lunch for a cigarette.

Don't get involved. It's all useless. They only screw you up.

If you feel left out or like you have to try them, go ahead, just remember that they will ruin your life in the long run.

Try, but don't use to extremes. Experimentation is normal but abuse is not.

Don't get messed up with drugs and alcohol—just bad news.

One word: Don't. I know this sounds like a commercial, but they won't get you anywhere.

Maybe they sound like fun, or feel like they are fun, but in the end all you become is a loser.

It's up to you, don't be stupid. They are a waste of time and nothing but trouble.

Wouldn't know and that's good.

Just say no!!

Be responsible.

Stay out of them. My friends and I had lots of fun, and we never got into them. There are many other things to do instead of drugs.

Don't do them—They will only hurt your body and your relationships—and it's way too easy to get addicted. They aren't worth it.

Alcohol and drugs may seem fun, but you end up looking and feeling stupid.

Don't party all weekend. Try just Friday night so you can recover from the hangover. Stay away from speed and anything harder than weed. Never drink on a Sunday night.

Stay as far away from these as possible. They can only ruin every single aspect of your life. All the things below will be ruined by alcohol and drugs.

Interestingly, most seniors in high school advise 8th-graders to avoid alcohol and drugs even though many of them have experimented themselves. The reward must not outweigh the risk.

FRIENDS

Get as many as possible, you never know when you'll need them.

Have lots of friends. Be a friend to everyone.

Have as many friends as you can. They will help you later in life.

Make as many as you can.

Numbers don't matter.

You can never have too many.

You'll change your freshman year, but don't let go of your friends. A true friend will always be there and stick by you through it all.

Get out of the cliques and be friends with everyone.

Be yourself. The world is more interesting with diversity. Be friends with everyone. Don't make enemies.

Hold on to them. They're very important.

Don't let your troubles with friends bring you down because you will laugh about it in a few years.

Keep your close friends. They are almost as important as family members when you are growing up.

It will take you a while to know who your true friends are, but I do promise one day you'll know. So for now only be yourself. Don't let him/her tell you what is cool or not. Only you can determine that. Walk around with high hopes and your head up. Smile and be yourself.

Hold on to your good friends because a good friend is more important than anything. Don't get caught up being friends with someone who is cool. Be friends with someone you truly like.

Friends get you through the rough times in high school. But when you are a senior, you get scared and think you may never see some of them again. Value it. Have fun.

Don't worry about making everyone like you. If you've got a couple good friends and can get along well with other people, you'll be fine.

Never hold a grudge with someone for more than a day or two. Your life in school is so short. It goes by before you know it. Be friends with everyone because it is such a short time. Also find a friend that you can share everything with.

Stay true to them, don't ditch them for someone (over a boyfriend or girlfriend).

Make good ones and keep them.

Your real friends will be with you forever—never give up on them.

Watch out. Some kids are snakes. Have friends you can trust.

Choose your friends wisely and don't ditch friends from Middle School because they might not be as "popular" as you in high school.

Have friends you can trust.

Just make more, don't lose any.

As many friends as you think you have, there is always room for more.

Get as many as you can.

Get a lot of them, you will need them.

Make lots of friends.

Be careful when you choose them.

Pick good friends that like to listen and talk too.

Be nice to everyone, it pays off when there's no "popular" group anymore.

This advice has always been divided into two camps. One camp says make as many friends as you can. The other says you only need one or a few good friends.

SCHOOL

Get as good grades as you can because you will appreciate that in not a very long future.

Study and pass classes, don't skip too much so you can enjoy the summer days at the end of the year.

Be serious about school, because an education is really important in our society, but there's more to life than school.

Study for yourself; get grades not for teachers, not for parents, but for yourself because you'll need this knowledge.

Stay in school and learn as much as you can because you're going to need it.

Strive to do well, but don't get stressed. If you love art—take the classes, don't hold yourself back because you need to take algebra.

Do your best. No matter how well you do, try. Then if you don't do as well as you had hoped, at least you know you put forth your best effort.

Get through it. It's better on the other side.

Keep up on school work. You may hate it, but there's no use failing, you'll just be in the school even longer. Always work hard because you can be anything you want to be as long as you try.

Stay there! The only way to get anywhere is just to finish.

Work hard. Grades should be your first priority. I wish I would've tried harder. You have the rest of your life to have fun.

Go to school and listen and do your work and graduate. It'll help you.

Stay in!! Don't skip class just because you can. You will want teachers to like you. Work your hardest—do your homework . . . but don't get overloaded.

Try your hardest. It's worth it in the end.

Don't procrastinate!!

Pay attention! Don't fool around! It may not seem important, but your whole future rests on what you do now.

It's your preparation for your future—work hard.

Have fun and work hard.

Do well in school; it will pay off in the future.

"A" students are not smarter than anybody else; they just spend more time doing homework.

Take it seriously.

Study more, work harder, I wish I had because it pays off in the end.

It's an experience everyone wishes they could go back and do again.

Learn to like it. It is fun. Look at what you learn besides school work.

Why not do your best? It's free now. You pay for college.

All you have in the end is your education.

Work hard because if you work hard now you will continue success all the way through your schooling.

Learn to like school and respect your teachers. Remember they are there for you.

It is hard to always do your best. Though school is very, very important, it's hard to realize just how important. Though, you'll know once you start thinking about colleges. So do your homework and listen in class no matter how boring you may think the teacher is and I promise you, you'll do just fine.

Do the best that you can in school, but know when to relax. Strive for your best, but don't get burned out in the process.

School is sure boring, but now that I'm a senior and I know that I will miss it and you get stressed thinking about college and who you are going to be.

Get all your credits out of the way in the first three years so you can slide your senior year.

Try your best at school. Don't make school hard. Take classes that you enjoy. Always have fun and make the best out of everything school life has to offer. Remember time flies by.

It's fun, make the best of it.

Make the most of it.

Pay attention, do well.

Stay in school!! Don't drop out!! Walk across that stage!!

Make it fun.

High school is a lot different than middle school. Don't smart off to older kids and you'll be fine.

Stay in school—it's worth the education.

Go home after school or sports. Do all your homework right away then go have fun.

Try hard, but don't lose your social life over it.

Do as much homework as possible so you can make as much as possible out of your life.

Stay in it. You'll need the money down the line.

Study!

Stay in it.

Work hard. It's worth it!!!

Don't screw off. Just do your work and get done.

Do your best, push yourself sometimes.

EXTRACURRICULARS

Don't limit yourself to school "stuff." Try to develop all skills you have so you'll be a complete person in life.

When someone tells you that you can be good in something, try it.

Stay in sports and try your hardest. Don't give up because you might need it in the long run.

Be involved! Drama is the best! Even if you are shy, go out for drama anyway—you'll get over it.

Get involved and stay involved. You'll stay out of trouble.

Do it if you want to.

Be known in everything you do.

Take extracurricular activities. There are memories to look back on.

Be in all the stuff you can because that's how you make more friends that will be with you forever.

Get involved!! There is no use to sitting on your butt!

Do them if you want. Don't let your parents make you. They are fun, but don't keep doing it if it's not fun.

Contrary to popular belief, the number of extracurriculars you do doesn't mean you are a better or worse person. If you hate something—quit! It's not worth it.

Join a lot. Things there help you meet new people and help out with real life problems.

Enjoy! Don't stress over it.

Get in as many as you can. They are fun and it helps when it comes to college.

Be in as many as you have time for! Try everything; it makes your life better.

Have fun and join them while you can.

Get involved! Drama, sports, yearbook, or anything else. . . . Just get involved. Your life will be more interesting if you do.

Do as many as possible. Sports are great for you. Play football.

Do what you want and do your best.

The best things happen during sports.

Participate in everything you can.

Good idea.

Get involved as much as you can. It looks good for college and it's fun.

It keeps you out of trouble and you make a lot of good friends. Try something *new*!!!

Join everything, but don't burn yourself out. Peer helpers, NHS, student council, sports/athletics, and drama. They're all great.

Get involved with as much as possible.

Do it, if only one sport or activity and make it fun.

I really wish I would have done sports.

Enjoy!!

Play sports or get involved. It makes high school a lot more fun.

Sports are very important to athletes. Remember if you are not an athlete that is all right. Just remember your priorities and school comes first!!

Get involved with activities that truly interest you because those activities can give you memories to last a lifetime.

Do them!! There are a lot of memories. The more you do, the more memories you make. It's hard to do it and smoke so try not to smoke.

Be in as many as you can handle. You make lots of friends.

Get involved with everything you can. Not just sports. Make every effort to have fun and meet people not just from your own school.

Sports are tough, but stay in them.

Give things a try at least.

Get involved, but only if you want to.

Stay in the sport you love!! Don't give up for dumb reasons.

Don't be afraid to try new things except crack and LSD.

Join everything you can—from any kind of sport, to NHS or Spanish club. These can only make your high school experience better.

Play sports.

Try everything. Keep doing what you like.

Do as many as possible.

Participate, you will be happier.

For sports, remember "there is no off-season"

Do as many as you can.

Try to play sports or get active in something. It's good!

Get involved. You don't have to be "good" to have fun and meet people.

BOYS/GIRLS

Things will happen in your life that you can't change, but it's no reason to shut out the world.

Relationships are important—but don't move from guy to guy or girl to girl. Friends are way more important than boy/girl friends.

Stay away!! They only ruin your life!!

Don't get too serious!!

Okay to have, but nothing too serious.

Like yourself before you like anyone else. Devote yourself to yourself. Don't give another a lot of power.

Do what you think is right.

They are not all bad. Just don't take relationships too seriously, I mean, this is just high school!

Have friends of both sexes because you need to be comfortable around boys/girls that you aren't going out with.

Don't have a boy/girlfriend. It's great to have someone there, but just a friend is better.

Wait for love.

You can have more friends than girlfriends.

Boy/girlfriends aren't all that important. Just have good friends of both sexes and it'll all work out okay.

Date a lot and get to know people, but hang on to your morals (like virginity)—it is something special to be saved for your true love.

Don't play a king, that you're the most important person on the earth who knows everything; first be a friend with them.

Relate with both sexes. Women need to be with men and men have a much better life if they have more than one girlfriend.

Enjoy it!! But don't do anything you'll regret.

Don't base your life on them.

Be yourself.

Don't get too involved with them too soon or else . . .

Go for it.

Don't even bother, but if you do, don't forget your friends.

Don't keep a girl/boy friend for too long—experience a lot.

Girls are crazy!!

Have someone you can trust.

When having a boy or girlfriend in high school, you have to learn to divide your time with friends and boy or girlfriends. If you ditch your friends too much for the boy/girl friend, you'll pay in the end.

Never let a boy/girl friend ruin your life. No one is worth it.

Be a gentleman. Be a lady.

Have fun, but don't do something you'll regret.

Make friends with the opposite sex before having a relationship. Never do things with them that you don't want to.

Two words—be careful.

Be careful, only have one at a time.

Girls can be the biggest witches or your best friends. Guys are great to have. They make you feel loved and don't let them walk all over you. (If any guy abuses you in any way, turn him in.)

Relationships are wonderful, but be careful because a bad one can really burn.

Okay, this is a big subject. I know at age 13, you think that your sweet-heart is the one you will marry. Don't get me wrong . . . you may. But most of the time it doesn't work like that. So keep your morals straight—I guess the best advice I can give you is abstinence!!!!

Have relationships that help you grow. Just don't think that if something goes wrong it's the end of the world.

Be respectful.

They are not always the best stress-relievers.

Don't have only boyfriends or girlfriends—have friends.

Have boyfriend or girlfriends, but don't give up on your friends. Be involved with everyone.

Yeah, things will change between you guys and girls. Your feelings will change, and you'll see each other in a whole new light. Don't be scared. It's great and fun.

Dating is fine. I recommend it, but don't get too serious with it.

Be careful about the ones who only want to use you and if you get dumped, it's their loss.

PARENTS

Parents are always there for you. You get mad at them when you are a teenager, but try to tolerate them. I regret some of the things I've said—just remember they are always there.

Be kind to your parents. They brought you into this world. If they don't let you do what you want it is because they love you. Have respect for them and they will have respect for you.

Respect them!!!!

Don't be so hard on them.

Listen to them unless they are drunks.

If parents nag you in high school, don't worry about it because they only want the best for you.

Listen to your parents. They have been around longer than you so they know what they're doing.

Work with them.

Be nice to them, they will help out.

Remember the Fourth Commandment.

Listen to them, they are not dumb.

Respect and obey your parents. Love them too!!

Tell the truth.

Love your parents. Turn to them when you need.

No comment. I don't live at home.

Learn to appreciate your parents, they'll mean a lot to you later. Remember that blood is thicker than water.

Respect and love them because they are the only reason why you are here.

Be friends with them. My mom is my best friend; try to be a friend with them, or at least with one of them.

Listen to your parents. They have good advice and can help you out.

Cut them some slack—they've been in your shoes and know what they're talking about—even if they seem "old-fashioned."

Try to get along with your parents. No matter how difficult it is to believe, most often they do know best. *Talk* to your parents!! Tell them what's going on in your life!!

Listen to them. They usually know what they are talking about.

Respect them. They are your safety belts.

Look up to your parents. They mean well and are just looking out for you.

Always be good to them, because they love you very much.

Listen to them, even if it feels like they are wrong, you find out that they were right in the end.

They will really bug you. Try to communicate with them. Don't get all mad and storm away. It will just make things worse. Work it out.

Being good pays off!! If you are good now, your parents will let you do more when you are older. Trust is invaluable.

Listen. Mom and dad know best.

Don't take them too seriously.

Behave, and don't tick them off so they kick you out. You'll need them later.

Try to have a relationship with them—they aren't that bad.

Parents really mean a lot and you never know how much you need them.

Be patient—things end up working out better if you can talk instead of yelling.

Respect them. Even if they tick you off, it's for a reason. They want to help you be a better person.

Listen and obey because they'll always be there.

It's hard to see eye to eye with your folks, but try because deep down they only want the best for you.

Respect your parents. They've raised you for a long time. Take care of them as they'll take care of you.

Try not to let them get you too ticked off because some day you are going to really miss them.

Don't argue—I don't and I'm rarely in trouble or rebel. My sister does and she's grounded a lot.

They only don't let you do something because they love you.

Give 'em a break. They've raised you and babied you for so long, now it's hard for them to let go.

Listen to them. They may have been stupid way back in 7/8th grades, but I understand them now.

They do know what they're talking about.

Be honest. If your parents trust you, they will let you have a lot of fun.

They know better than you, but don't always let that stop you.

Listen to them.

As hard as this may be to believe, your parents are your best friends! They will always, always be there for you through anything. So appreciate them and they will trust you and respect you as their child.

TEACHERS

They are excellent . . . some are hard to handle, but they will respect you if you respect them.

Some are good. Some are bad. Work with them whatever they're like.

Get to know at least one teacher well.

They're okay—you get some good ones, you get some bad ones.

At the high school there are some goons, and some that are so crabby and mean, but there are others that are so great. Give 'em all a chance.

Teachers try—just be understandable and pay attention and you will graduate.

Definitely classy people.

Respect them. They are there to help you.

Be respectful because their job is hard too. Don't get too worked up if they make you mad, it's only school.

They are the smartest people you'll ever know, so listen to all they try to teach you.

Don't get lippy. Pay attention to them. They really are people. In fact they can become your best friends.

There are a few grade-"stingy" ones, but try and talk to them, not swear and yell, and they might listen.

Teachers help you in more ways than you can know. If you can read this, thank a teacher.

They are here to help you—not ruin your life.

Get as many teachers to like you as you can.

Respect them.

Listen to them, they have been doing this for awhile and know what they are talking about.

If you want, lower yourself to kiss up. It works.

Cherish them. There are seldom teachers that you can really connect with.

Listen to them because they actually know what they're talking about.

Get along with the teachers. They don't put up with anything. So treat them well.

Don't burn bridges. You never know when you'll need a hand.

Treat them the same as parents.

Respect your teachers and stay ahead of the game. Keep up with your work.

Same deal as parents—listen to what they have to say.

Learn a lot from them, but consider also that they can make a lot of mistakes.

Respect them. *Listen.*

Be nice and obey them! They are great for the most part!!

Do what they say and you'll be fine.

Be nice to them, they will help out.

Talk to them and they can help you.

Give them what they want and they'll leave you alone.

Make friends with your teachers.

Respect your teachers even if you don't like them—it takes a lot for them to teach people like us.

Respect them, but don't believe everything. Question them.

Respect them.

Show respect for them and they will return it. Teachers don't give you hard work because they want to; it is because they want you to learn.

IF I COULD CHANGE ONE THING ABOUT MY JH/HS EXPERIENCE, I WOULD

Not smoke and don't have too many serious relationships.

I wish I would have done my assignments when they were due.

Get involved in drama.

Leave drugs alone, and keep my virginity.

Nothing. I learned from all my mistakes in junior high.

Not trying drama until my senior year.

Nothing.

I would have worked harder during the summer for sports.

Study more and hang out with friends less.

I would have been more responsible about my alcohol experiences and drug experiences.

Not drink so much. It was the best years except for that.

Take more chances.

Make some friends that I could trust with anything. Of course, I have friends, but it's always nice to have friends you can count on anytime, rain or shine.

Nothing.

I wish I concentrated more on school.

I never would have had a boyfriend.

I would have been in more extracurriculars because I wasn't very involved.

I wouldn't make as big of a deal out of petty arguments.

I would have done better in school. I should've got all A's.

I would change nothing.

Be my own person.

Do your homework.

I'd have stayed in more extracurriculars, otherwise, nothing!!

I wish I would have tried harder at my grades.

Not worry so much.

Be more assertive with people. If someone tells you to do something you don't want to do, don't do it.

Make sure that I didn't take anything for granted because I'll never get it back.

Be nice to absolutely everybody.

I would have worked harder on my schoolwork.

I would have done sports and gotten along better with my parents.

I would have joined extracurriculars earlier.

Nothing. Making mistakes in high school life are important! You learn from them. Trust me.

I would change nothing. It was great while it lasted, and now it's almost over, and I'll miss high school.

Not have started smoking, spent more time on schoolwork, applied for scholarships.

Study habits.

Nothing. I had an awesome time!!

Chapter Ten

Zap 19

Zap 19 is a futures project that I designed as part of my master's degree. I use it in my 8th-grade social studies class as a project. In my research, I found that the project had a significant effect on the student's "desire to achieve in school." I found it to be a useful tool in spurring discussions about the future. Having your child fill it out can create some great discussion at home.

ZAP 19: A LOOK INTO THE FUTURE

You are now either thirteen, fourteen, or fifteen years old. What will your life be like in five to six years? Many of the actions and decisions that you make now will affect your future, so why not think about them now? Below are three areas that will affect your life when you are nineteen. Your job is to research these areas to find possible solutions. Use any and all means to find this information including parents, employers, older brothers and sisters, social agencies, teachers, resources in any library, or *any* other resources you can possibly think of to help you collect the information that you need. You will answer every question and list a source for *every* bit of information that you give.

CATEGORY 1:
Economics/Career Decisions

A) Where will you live?

        Home?   +Will there be a rent charge? _____

Source_____

                 +Will you have to buy your
                     own food?

                 If yes, what are the monthly
                     costs?   _____

Source_____

      Apartment? +Average monthly rent?   _____

Source_____

                 +How much will you pay
                     for utilities?

                                  Heat   _____

                                  Water   _____

                                  Electricity _____

                                  Telephone _____

Source_____

                 +How much will furniture
                     cost?   _____

Source_____

                 +How will you wash your
                     clothes?   _____

                       Laundromat costs?   _____

Source_____

+How much will food cost
  per month?   _____

Source_____

College?

+How much is the average
  monthly stay for room and
  board at a college or
  university?   _____

Source_____

Buy a home?

+Average cost of a home?   _____

Source_____

+Bank finance charges for
  purchase?   _____

Source_____

+Monthly house payment?   _____

Source_____

+Monthly insurance payment? _____

Source_____

+Monthly property tax
  payment?   _____

Source_____

+How much for utilities?

         Heat   _____

         Water _____

Electricity   _____

Telephone   _____

Source_____

+How much for food?   _____

Source_____

+If you are moving to a
    different area of the state
    or nation, find the cost to
    move your possessions by
    a moving company.   _____

Source_____

B) How will you earn money?

Get living expenses from parents/guardians?

+How much are they willing
    or able to help you?   _____

Source_____

+For how long are they
    willing to help you?   _____

Source_____

+Will they pay for *all* living
    expenses, including food?
    If not, what costs will be
    up to you?   _____

Source_____

Get a job right out of high school?

+What kinds of job can a high
    school graduate get? Name
    the job you could get and

report the following
information about that
position.

Source_____

+How much will it pay?

    Per hour?   _____

    Per month?   _____

    Per year?   _____

+How many hours are you
    guaranteed?   _____

+Will you get benefits?

    Health insurance?   _____

    Life insurance?   _____

    Dental insurance?   _____

    Paid vacation?   _____

Source_____

If no to the above four, how
    much would it cost to buy
    privately?

    Health insurance?   _____

    Life insurance?   _____

    Dental insurance?   _____

    Paid vacation?   _____

Source_____

Work part-time while attending school?

    +Type of job?   _____

    +Where?   _____

    +Pay?   _____

+Hours?   _____

+Benefits? (If you are a
 student, your benefits
 may still be covered under
 your parent's insurance.)   _____

Source_____

Apply for General Assistance (otherwise
known as welfare)?

+Will GA run out? If so,
 when?   _____

+How much per month?   _____

+Are you required to be in
 school or looking for
 work?   _____

Source_____

*Get and fill out a job application based upon your qualifications
at this time.*

Careers

List three jobs you are interested in, their average salary in your
region, training needed, and the availability of jobs.

1)   Job title   _____

     Average salary   _____

     Training needed   _____

     Availability of jobs   _____

2)   Job title   _____

     Average salary   _____

     Training needed   _____

     Availability of jobs   _____

3)   Job title   _____

     Average salary   _____

     Training needed   _____

     Availability of jobs   _____

CATEGORY 2:
Academic Decisions

Will you go to a technical/community college, university, or
college?

> Two-year technical/community college?
> > +What would you study?   _____
> > +Where? (name of a school)   _____
> > +What are the minimum
> >   academic qualifications?   _____
> > > G.P.A.   _____
> > > Class rank   _____
> > > ACT/SAT score   _____

Source_____   _____

> > +How much does it cost?
> > > Tuition?   _____
> > > Fees?   _____
> > > Books?   _____

Source_____   _____

> > +How will you pay for it
> >   (loans, parents, work)?   _____

Source_____

Four-year public university?

      +What would you study?   _____

      +Where? (name of a school)   _____

      +What are the minimum
         academic qualifications?

            G.P.A.   _____

            Class rank   _____

            ACT/SAT score   _____

Source_____

      +How much does it cost?

            Tuition?   _____

            Fees?   _____

            Books?   _____

Source_____

      +How will you pay for it
         (loans, parents, work)?   _____

Source_____

Four-year private college?

      +What would you study?   _____

      +Where? (name of a school)   _____

      +What are the minimum
         academic qualifications?

            G.P.A.   _____

            Class rank   _____

            ACT/SAT score   _____

Source_____

+How much does it cost?

    Tuition? _____

    Fees? _____

    Books? _____

Source_____

+How will you pay for it
(loans, parents, work)? _____

Source_____

Four-year college/university and professional school
(to become a doctor, dentist, lawyer, etc.)?

+What would you study? _____

+Where? (name of a school) _____

+What are the minimum
academic qualifications?

    G.P.A. _____

    Class rank _____

    ACT/SAT score _____

Source_____

+How much does it cost?

    Tuition? _____

    Fees? _____

    Books? _____

Source_____

+How will you pay for it
(loans, parents, work)? _____

Source_____

* Get and fill out a college or technical school application based upon your qualifications at this time.

CATEGORY 3:
Personal Decisions

Alcohol

+Will you use alcohol? Why or why not?
   If yes, how much?

_____

+Find information about how much the average
   social drinker spends per year on alcohol
   consumption.   _____

Source_____

+Find out from a person who is/was an alcoholic
   or knows an alcoholic how much they spend
   per year on alcohol costs.   _____

Source_____

+What does alcohol do to the body? What short-
   and long-term effects does it have on the:

         Brain _____

         _____

         Heart _____

         _____

         Liver _____

         _____

Source_____

+Can you die from alcoholism? If yes: How? _____

_____

_____

Source_____

+What is the difference between a nondrinker,
a social drinker, someone who abuses alcohol,
and someone who is an alcoholic?

_____

Source_____

+Do you have a family history of
alcoholism? _____

Source_____

+Is it true that the earlier you use alcohol, the greater
your chances are of abusing it or of becoming
an alcoholic?

_____

Source_____

+Name at least five sources of help if you or someone
you know is struggling with alcohol use:

Name of agency or person   Address or phone #

1) _____   _____

2) _____   _____

3) _____   _____

4) _____   _____

5) _____   _____

Source_____

Drugs

+Do you plan to use drugs or not?   _____

+What is the illegal drug most widely used in
   the U.S. by teenagers at this time?   _____

Source_____

+Answer the following questions about each
   of the drugs listed:

Marijuana

1) What effect does it have on the body?

   Short-term _____

   Long-term _____

2) Is it addictive? If yes, how addictive is it?

   _____

   _____

3) Is it considered a "gateway" drug, opening the
   door to other drug use?

   _____

Source_____

Cocaine

1) What effect does it have on the body?

   Short-term _____

   _____

   Long-term _____

   _____

2) Is it addictive? If yes, how addictive is it?

_____

_____

3) Is it considered a "gateway" drug, opening the
   door to other drug use? _____

Source_____

Crack Cocaine

1) What effect does it have on the body?

Short-term _____

Long-term _____

2) Is it addictive? If yes, how addictive is it?

_____

_____

3) Is it considered a "gateway" drug, opening the
   door to other drug use? _____

Source_____

LSD (Hallucinogens)

1) What effect does it have on the body?

Short-term _____

_____

Long-term _____

_____

2) Is it addictive? If yes, how addictive is it?

_____

_____

3) Is it considered a "gateway" drug, opening the
door to other drug use? _____

Source_____

Amphetamines and Methamphetamines (Uppers)

1) What effect does it have on the body?

Short-term _____

_____

Long-term _____

_____

2) Is it addictive? If yes, how addictive is it?

_____

_____

3) Is it considered a "gateway" drug, opening the
door to other drug use? _____

Source_____

Barbiturates and Depressants (Downers)

1) What effect does it have on the body?

Short-term _____

_____

Long-term _____

_____

2) Is it addictive? If yes, how addictive is it?

_____

_____

3) Is it considered a "gateway" drug, opening the
door to other drug use? _____

Source_____

Angel Dust (PCP)

1) What effect does it have on the body?

Short-term _____

_____

Long-term _____

_____

2) Is it addictive? If yes, how addictive is it?

_____

_____

3) Is it considered a "gateway" drug, opening the
door to other drug use? _____

Source_____

Tobacco

+Are you planning to smoke or chew
tobacco? _____

+How much money does it cost to smoke two
packs of cigarettes a day at today's price
for one year? _____

Source_____

+What effect does tobacco use have on the body?

Heart _____

_____

Lungs _____

_____

Other organs affected? How? _____

_____

_____

Source_____

+What do you see as the image of a smoker? Is it cool
or repulsive or somewhere in the middle? Why?

_____

_____

_____

Married, Single

+Are you going to get married or stay single? Why?

_____

_____

_____

+How many children do you want to have? Why?

_____

_____

_____

+At what age do you want to have children? Why?

_____

_____

_____

Sex

+Name five sexually transmitted diseases and their
effects on the body.

1) _____

_____

2) _____

_____

3) _____

_____

4) _____

_____

5) _____

_____

Source_____

+ Is there a connection between teenage pregnancy and
annual income?

If yes, explain. _____

_____

_____

Source_____

+ What percentage of teenagers involved in a
teenage pregnancy get married and stay together?

_____

_____

Source_____

+ What percentage of teenagers who get pregnant:

Keep their baby?   _____

Give their baby up for adoption?   _____

Have an abortion?   _____

Source_____

The last part of this assignment is a personal letter to yourself based upon the very personal decision you make regarding the moral decision of when or if you will begin to be sexually active. Explain, in your letter, the age or time that you have chosen and explain why that age or time was chosen. For example, if you have chosen to wait until after marriage, explain why you have made this choice. If you are already sexually active, explain why you will continue to be, or why you will make the choice to stop. This portion of Zap 19 will not be handed in to the teacher.

Appendix

APPENDIX, SECTION 1:
Grade Contract

I, _____, agree and promise to work hard, ask questions, study for tests, and complete homework on time for _____ class. I agree that there should be rewards for a good grade (A or B) and consequences for a poor grade (D, F, or Incomplete). I am a partner in setting these rewards and consequences.

Grade	Reward/Consequence
A or B	_____
	_____
D, F, or I	_____
	_____

Signed,   Date

Student   _____   _____

Parent(s) _____   _____

_____   _____

APPENDIX, SECTION 2A:
"Bad Kid" Worksheet

Parent

1. Define "bad kid."

2. What do "bad kids" do that makes them "bad"?

3. Why does it make them "bad"?

4. What can my child do to avoid becoming a "bad kid" or becoming friends with a "bad kid"?

5. What can I do to help my child with this potential problem?

APPENDIX, SECTION 2B:
"Bad Kid" Worksheet

Student

1. Define "bad kid."

2. What do "bad kids" do that makes them "bad"?

3. Why does it make them "bad"?

4. What can I do to avoid becoming a "bad kid" or becoming friends with a "bad kid"?

5. What can my parents do to help me avoid this potential problem?

APPENDIX, SECTION 3:
Smoking Cigarettes

I, _____, promise that I will not smoke cigarettes. If I do smoke, the following consequences, which I came up with and agree to, will be put into action:

1. _____

2. _____

3. _____

_____   _____
Daughter/Son   Date

_____   _____
Parent(s)   Date

APPENDIX, SECTION 4:
Drugs, Alcohol, Tobacco, and Other Chemicals Worksheet

1. What kinds of chemicals do people use?

	Chemical	Short-term effect	Long-term effect
A.	_____	_____	_____
B.	_____	_____	_____
C.	_____	_____	_____
D.	_____	_____	_____
E.	_____	_____	_____
F.	_____	_____	_____

2. Why do people use chemicals?

3. What is addiction?

4. What good things can happen when you use chemicals?

5. What bad things can happen when you use chemicals?

APPENDIX, SECTION 5:
Contract: Drugs, Alcohol, or Other Chemicals

I, _____, agree and promise that I will not use drugs, alcohol, or any other chemical.

If I am in a position where I feel pressured or threatened to use them, my parents will provide a ride for me anytime/anywhere. They agree that they will not lecture me or be angry with me at the time, but a serious conversation will be held the following day.

_____   _____

Daughter/Son   Date

_____   _____

Parent(s)   Date

APPENDIX, SECTION 6:
Contract: Drugs, Alcohol, or Other Chemicals and Cars

I, _____, agree and promise that I will not drive after drinking or ride with anyone who has been drinking or using any other chemical.

If I am in a position where I feel pressured or threatened to ride or drive after drinking or using any other chemical, my parents will provide a ride for me anytime/anywhere. They agree that they will not lecture me or be angry with me at the time, but a serious conversation will be held the following day.

_____   _____
Daughter/Son   Date

_____   _____
Parent(s)   Date

APPENDIX, SECTION 7:
Friend Form

Date became friends _____

Name _____

Address _____

Phone number _____

Name(s) of parent(s) _____   _____

Things in common:

_____

_____

_____

Common friends:

_____   _____

_____   _____

APPENDIX, SECTION 8:
Put-down Worksheet

1. What does it feel like to be bullied?

2. What does it feel like to bully?

3. What is empathy and why is it important?

4. What is a bully?

5. What should you do if someone is bullying you verbally?

6. What should you do if someone is bullying you physically?

7. Should you stick up for someone else if they are being bullied?

APPENDIX, SECTION 9:
Bullying Contract

I promise to tell my parents/guardians immediately if someone is bullying me. We will make a plan together to take care of the problem.

_____	_____
Daughter/Son	Date
_____	_____
Parent(s)	Date

APPENDIX, SECTION 10:
Behavior Contract

I, _____, agree that positive behavior is expected in school. It is my duty to act respectfully and responsibly. If I break school or teacher rules, I could receive any or all of the following consequences:

1. _____

2. _____

3. _____

4. _____

5. _____

6. _____

7. _____

The above consequences are reasonable, and I agree to follow through with them if needed.

_____   _____
Daughter/Son   Date

_____   _____
Parent(s)   Date

APPENDIX, SECTION 11:
Student Daily Planner, Week of _____

Assignments	Monday	Tuesday	Wednesday	Thursday	Friday
1st Hour	_____	_____	_____	_____	_____
2nd Hour	_____	_____	_____	_____	_____
3rd Hour	_____	_____	_____	_____	_____
4th Hour	_____	_____	_____	_____	_____
5th Hour	_____	_____	_____	_____	_____
6th Hour	_____	_____	_____	_____	_____
7th Hour	_____	_____	_____	_____	_____

Plan for after school:

2:30–3:30	_____
3:30–4:30	_____
4:30–5:30	_____
5:30–6:30	_____
6:30–7:30	_____
7:30–8:30	_____
8:30–9:30	_____

Big projects I found out about this week:

Class	Project	Due Date
_____	_____	_____
_____	_____	_____
_____	_____	_____

APPENDIX, SECTION 12:
Friend for Life Contract

I, _____, promise that if one of the people on
my contract ever tell me that they are going to attempt suicide, I
will immediately tell an adult. If I suspect that they are a danger to
another person, I will also tell an adult.

_____

My signature

_____   _____   _____

Friend for Life   Friend for Life   Friend for Life

_____   _____   _____

Friend for Life   Friend for Life   Friend for Life

APPENDIX, SECTION 13:
Parent/Child Anti-Suicide Contract

I, _____, promise to tell my parents/guardians if
I am thinking about hurting myself. I also promise to tell my
parents if one of my friends has told me that they are going to hurt
themselves. As parents, we promise to handle the situation with
care and concern by seeking professional help or by reporting the
friend's actions or behaviors to a school counselor.

_____   _____

Student Signature   Parent Signature

APPENDIX, SECTION 14:
Useful Resources for Parents and Teens

Books

Bowman, Susan, Ed.S., LPC, and Kaye Randall, LMSW. *See My Pain: Creative Strategies and Activities for Helping Young People Who Self-Injure.*

Byars, Betsy, ed. *Classic Teen Stories.*

Canfield, Jack, et al. *Chicken Soup for the Teenage Soul.*

Carlson, Richard. *Don't Sweat the Small Stuff for Teens.*

Cobain, Bev. *When Nothing Matters Anymore: A Survival Guide for Depressed Teens.*

Costin, Carolyn. *The Eating Disorder Sourcebook: A Comprehensive Guide to the Causes, Treatments, and Prevention of Eating Disorders.*

Cudney, Milton R., and Robert E. Hardy. *Self-Defeating Behaviors: Free Yourself from the Habits, Compulsions, Feelings, and Attitudes That Hold You Back.*

Dellasega, Cheryl. *Girl Wars: 12 Strategies That Will End Female Bullying.*

Dellasega, Cheryl. *Surviving Ophelia: Mothers Share Their Wisdom in Navigating the Tumultuous Teenage Years.*

Elkind, David. *The Hurried Child: Growing Up Too Fast Too Soon.*

Flick, Grad L. *How to Reach and Teach Teenagers with ADHD*.

Freedman, Judy S. *Easing the Teasing: Helping Your Child Cope with Name-Calling, Ridicule, and Verbal Bullying*.

Friel, John C., Ph.D. *The Seven Best Things Smart Teens Do*.

Gordon, Sol, Ph.D. *When Living Hurts: For Teenagers, Young Adults, their Parents, Leaders, and Counselors*.

Gurian, Michael. *The Minds of Boys: Saving Our Sons from Falling Behind in School and Life*.

Kindlon, Dan. *Raising Cain: Protecting the Emotional Life of Boys*.

Levenkron, Steven. *Cutting: Understanding and Overcoming Self-Mutilation*.

McGraw, Jay. *Daily Life Strategies for Teens*.

Nikkah, John. *Our Boys Speak: Adolescent Boys Write About Their Inner Lives*.

Pelzer, Dave. *Help Yourself for Teens: Real-Life Advice for Real-Life Challenges*.

Pipher, Mary. *Real Boys: Rescuing Our Sons from the Myths of Boyhood*.

Pipher, Mary. *Reviving Ophelia: Saving the Selves of Adolescent Girls*.

Rutledge, Jill Zimmerman. *Dealing with the Stuff That Makes Life Tough: The 10 Things That Stress Teen Girls Out and How to Cope with Them*.

Shandler, Sara. *Ophelia Speaks: Adolescent Girls Write About Their Search for Self.*

Simmons, Rachel. *Odd Girl Out: The Hidden Culture of Aggression in Girls.*

Simmons, Rachel. *Odd Girl Speaks Out: Girls Write about Bullies, Cliques, Popularity, and Jealousy.*

Snyderman, Nancy L. *Girl in the Mirror: Mothers and Daughters in the Years of Adolescence.*

Strauch, Barbara. *The Primal Teen: What the New Discoveries About the Teenage Brain Tell Us About Our Kids.*

Strong, Marilee. *A Bright Red Scream: Self-Mutilation and the Language of Pain.*

Thompson, Michael. *Best Friends, Worst Enemies: Understanding the Social Lives of Children.*

Walsh, David. *WHY Do They Act That Way?: A Survival Guide to the Adolescent Brain for You and Your Teen.*

Weill, Sabrina. *The Real Truth about Teens and Sex: From Hooking Up to Friends with Benefits—What Teens Are Thinking, Doing, and Talking About, and How to Help Them Make Smart Choices.*

Websites

www.psychologymatters.com
www.positiveparenting.com
www.parenting.com
www.parenthood.com

www.parenting.org
www.familyeducation.com
www.practicalparenting.org
www.parentingadolescents.com
www.parentingtoolbox.com
www.educationworld.com/standards/
    (national and state education standards)
www.ldonline.org
    (learning disabilities)
www.helendowland.terminus.net
    (gifted children)
www.nagc.org
    (gifted children)
www.drugabuse.gov
    (National Institute on Drug Abuse)
www.focusas.com
    (drug and alcohol issues)
www.fbi.gov/publications/pguide/pguidee.htm
    (Internet safety)
www.bullyonline.org
    (cyber bullying)
www.stopcyberbullying.org
    (cyber bullying)

About the Author

Glen Gilderman lives in Duluth, Minnesota, with his wife, Terrie, and his two children Katie, age fourteen, and Boston, age ten. He has been a teacher since 1987, the last fourteen years working with 7th-, 8th-, and 9th-grade middle school social studies students for the Proctor Public Schools in Proctor, Minnesota. Prior to that, he worked as a special education teacher in many different settings. He has a bachelor's degree from the College of Saint Scholastica and a master's degree from the University of Wisconsin–Superior. Being a middle school teacher and parent, he brings a dual perspective to teaching middle school students and working with their parents.